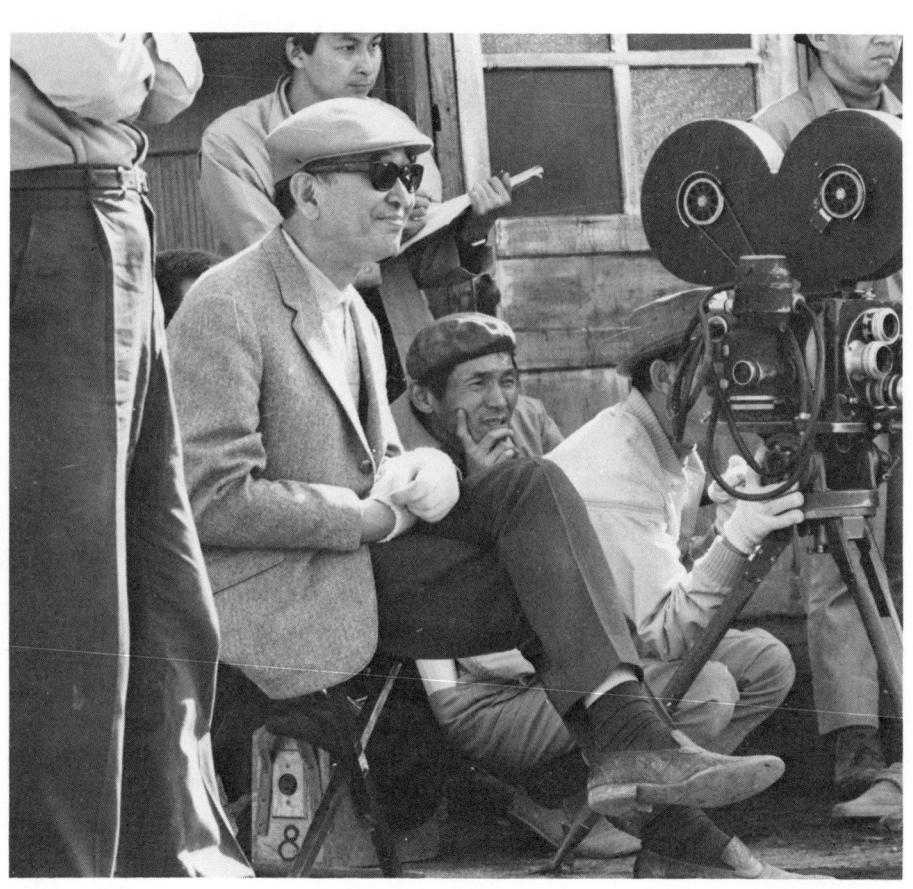

Akira
KUROSAWA

*a guide to
references and resources*

*A
Reference
Publication
in
Film*

Ronald Gottesman
Editor

Akira KUROSAWA

a guide to references and resources

PATRICIA ERENS

G.K. HALL &CO.
70 LINCOLN STREET, BOSTON, MASS.

Copyright © 1979 by Patricia Erens

Library of Congress Cataloging in Publication Data
Erens, Patricia, 1938-
  Akira Kurosawa: a guide to references and resources.

  (A Reference publication in film)
  Includes indexes.
  1. Kurosawa, Akira, 1910- — Bibliography.
I. Series.
Z8468.62.E73   [PN1998.A3K78]   016.79143'0233'0924
ISBN 0-8161-7994-8   78-11501

This publication is printed on permanent/durable acid-free paper
MANUFACTURED IN THE UNITED STATES OF AMERICA

For Jay
who was always there

Contents

Preface. xi
Biographical Background. 1
Critical Survey of Oeuvre 13
The Films: Synopsis, Credits and Notes. 31
Writings about Akira Kurosawa, 1951-1977. 71
Performances and Writings 119
Archival Sources 123
Film Distributors 127
Author Index 129
Film Title Index 133

Preface

The information included in this manuscript represents a thorough research of materials in English, French, and Japanese. The documentation in English and French is complete within the limits cited below. The Japanese materials are selective only, due to the inaccessibility of many journals and newspapers. I have included, however, the most important books and articles written by Japan's foremost film scholars. In general, newspaper articles and reviews are not listed, although an indication of the Japanese response to individual films appears in the biographical section on Kurosawa.

French reviews for Kurosawa films are taken almost exclusively from film journals. For English language reviews, however, I have included articles from the popular press. With regard to newspapers, citations are limited for the most part to *The New York Times, The Village Voice,* and *Variety. The New York Times* was chosen because of its accessibility and broad distribution; *The Village Voice* because of the prestige of its reviewers; and *Variety* because of its influence upon distribution.

Except in two cases, all films were screened personally. I was not able to see *One Wonderful Sunday* (1947) or *Those Who Make Tomorrow* (1946). The precis for *One Wonderful Sunday* was drawn from the published scenario which includes all technical directions. Information on *Those Who Make Tomorrow* was taken from a German text provided by the Oesterreichisches Filmmuseum in Vienna.

In an effort to establish uniformity and clarity, all film titles have been standardized in English in accordance with the names most frequently used by reviewers. Thus *Seven Samurai* (1954) is used throughout despite the fact the film was first released in the U.S. as *The Magnificent Seven* and is often referred to as *The Seven Samurai.* All French, Japanese and variant titles which appeared as part of an article or as review headings are cited in the original in the annotated bibliography, but all notations are rendered in the standardized version. The index cross-references all titles.

In the annotated bibliography entries are arranged chronologically by year of publication and are then alphabetized under the name of the author, editor, or translator. Reprints are also included and are listed under the author's name by reprint date. The reprinted entry is not annotated. A cross-reference, however, will lead the user to the original entry. Unseen entries are flagged with an asterisk.

In the case of anthologies or special magazine issues, an entry appears under the name of the editor, citing the scope of the work and the names of individual contributors. Each article is then annotated separately under the name of the author, and listed alphabetically within the year.

In a few instances where books have gone into second editions or been republished later in paperback, new entries are included with cross-references. Journals which overlap a two-year period (e.g. 1956-1957), have been entered under the earlier date.

Japanese titles are rendered in transliteration rather than in the original Japanese characters. English translations appear in brackets. No translations are provided for French titles as, in most cases, their meanings are readily apparent. Publication information for foreign entries, however, is given in English.

In Japan, names are written with the surname listed first. This order has been maintained in the listing of Japanese materials. However, for all other entries (plot synopses, credits, and annotations), I have used the English format with the given name listed first. In translating character names from Japanese into English, spellings sometimes vary. Alternate spellings are listed in the credits. In a few instances authorities differ and characters are referred to by totally different names. These discrepancies are also noted in the credits. In addition, most materials relating to Japanese films (including English subtitles) refer to male characters by their surname and female characters by their given name. Although I would have liked to eliminate such sexual discrimination in the plot synopses, the volume of published material which follows this tradition would make change difficult and lead to possible confusion.

My gratitude extends to Donald Richie, who was most helpful on this project and whose book, *The Films of Akira Kurosawa*, remains the most complete English-language resource. Its existence has saved me innumerable hours of research.

I am also extremely grateful to Robert O. Dehnsohn, Michio Takeda, Leah Maneaty, Gretchen Bisplinghoff and David Owens who all spent long hours in the preparation of the Japanese and French texts and to Tomoko Takeuchi and Noboru Kohsaka who gathered materials in Tokyo.

Lastly, I am indebted to both Luz Campos and Christy Marvin who helped in the research and preparation of the manuscript.

I would also like to thank the following people for allowing me to screen prints and for providing me with material necessary for the preparation of this book:

Linda Artel	Pacific Film Archives
Brenda Davis	British Film Institute
Dorothy Desmond	Audio-Brandon Films
Yoichi Matsue	Assistant to Mr. Kurosawa

Kazuto Ohira	Toho International, (USA) Inc.
Jerry Rappaport	International Film Exchange
Patrick Sheehan	Motion Picture Division, Library of Congress
Akira Shimizu	Japan Film Library Council
Charles Silver	Film Study Center — Museum of Modern Art
Yukinobu Toba	National Film Center — Tokyo

Also, thanks go to Ronald Gottesman, Elizabeth Kubik, and Barbara Garrey for their encouragement and patience and for advice on the editing and final version of this book.

Biographical Background

The facts of Kurosawa's life are sparse and simple. He is an extremely private man and has granted few interviews during his lifetime. His close friends are his co-workers and except on rare occasions he has remained out of the limelight. In truth, Kurosawa's life is the history of his films. Therefore, the following biography will deal in the main with the production, filming, and reception of Kurosawa's works and the influence these events had on his thinking and feeling. The information pertaining to Kurosawa's early life and career are drawn from an article which he wrote in 1963, published in Tokyo. Facts on the various film projects are from articles and interviews, especially those written by Donald Richie.

Akira Kurosawa was born on March 23, 1910, in Tokyo. He was the youngest of seven children in a family which consisted of four boys and three girls. His parents were both natives of Tokyo. His father, Isamu Kurosawa, was a graduate of the first class at Toyama School, a military academy. A severe man, he was committed to the concept of physical fitness and pushed all his sons in this direction. He earned a middling income by teaching at the Ebara Middle School.

As a child Kurosawa was weak and has referred to himself as a cry-baby. He neither participated in sports nor was motivated to earn high grades. For awhile he considered himself backward. During his second year in primary school the family moved and he transferred to the Kuroda Primary School at Edogawa. It was here that he first met Keinosuke Uegusa, who later became a scriptwriter and close collaborator on such films as *One Wonderful Sunday* (1947) and *Drunken Angel* (1948).

Kurosawa's primary school teacher, a man named Tachikawa, became the first major influence on his life. Because of Tachikawa's interest in fine arts, he developed the boy's sensitivity toward visual expression. Kurosawa's father proved surprisingly supportive of these new ventures.

Graduating to the Keika High School, Kurosawa was required to take compulsory military training, but his natural aversion to guns and shooting made him a poor student in this field. During his last year in high school he enrolled in art classes at the Doshusha School of Western Painting.

Kurosawa excelled in his new studies and his works were twice selected for inclusion in the Nika-kai Art Association Show, a modern exhibition established to oppose the traditional government supported art. In 1927 Kurosawa graduated from high school and decided to devote his life to painting.

Unhappily he soon discovered that he could not support himself and turned to doing posters and illustrations for ladies' magazines. He joined the Japan Proletariat Artist's Group which advocated Marxist theories, became an avid reader, and developed an interest in Russian literature, especially for the works of Fedor Dostoyevsky and Maxim Gorky. The works of these authors would remain a passion throughout his lifetime.

Kurosawa has commented on this stage of his life in an interview with Joan Mellen. He states, "In my youth the situation of society was much worse than it is now. I experienced being a sort of Marxist. It was very fashionable among the youth. For one thing, we couldn't get jobs after graduation from the university. There was a fever among young people. They did not know how to use their energies. I would say that almost all the intellectual urban youth in that period were at one time or another Marxists. They were not satisfied with the government and its policies. I was one of them. In reflection, we were also enjoying the thrill of being Marxists. But it is doubtful that I was a true Marxist, although I had that tendency."[1]

Kurosawa dropped out of the Marxist movement because of ill health and spent the following year in bed. By the time he recovered, the movement had been dispersed and many of the primary agitators were under arrest.

During this same period Kurosawa became very close with his third brother, Heigo. Heigo was artistic and loved films. Their relationship provided the second major influence on Kurosawa's life. Because of Heigo's Bohemian lifestyle and premarital affair with a young woman, the elder Kurosawa cut off relations with his son. The two brothers stayed in close contact, however.

Heigo worked as a *benshi* (interpreter of silent films) in movie theaters and thus was able to obtain free passes. He often took Kurosawa to the movies and afterward the two spent long hours talking. When Heigo committed suicide at the age of twenty, his loss was a major blow to Kurosawa.

By 1936 Kurosawa had still not settled into any kind of permanent work. Although his interest in film was great, he had not seriously thought of film as a career. However, when the P.C.L. (Photo-Chemical Laboratory, later Toho Motion Picture Company), placed an advertisement in the newspaper for assistant directors, Kurosawa responded. The ad requested applicants to submit an essay detailing the defects of the Japanese cinema and suggesting ways for improvement. Of the 800 respondents, approximately 500 were called to the studio. There they were asked to write a treatment from a newspaper clipping. Those who passed (seven in number) were given a personal interview. At this session Kajiro Yamamoto, who later became Kurosawa's mentor, remembered being impressed with the young man's knowledge of art. Kurosawa was hired along with four others and began work.

The studio, only two years old, was a perfect place for a young ambitious man like Kurosawa. More open and free thinking than other companies, it provided room to experiment and move ahead. At first, however, Kurosawa was disenchanted. Then after an assignment to Yamamoto's unit, the whole world of film possibilities opened up. Yamamoto became his teacher and model.

Yamamoto's method of filming was to involve everyone in the process of production. Extremely generous with his time and attention, he always encouraged the younger men in his unit. During this period Kurosawa began writing scenarios, a common practice for assistant directors. He worked hard, wrote quickly and was extremely prolific. Yamamoto has commented that Kurosawa had a natural talent and even his most casual work was inspired. Behind this frenzy was a desire to direct his own films. For this, however, the young assistant director would have to wait several years.

Kurosawa worked on several Yamamoto films, including *The Loves of Tojuro* (1938) and *Composition Class* (1938). At this period he renewed acquaintances with Uegusa who was now at the Photo-Chemical Laboratory working as an extra. Kurosawa's most important work under Yamamoto came with the filming of *Horses* (1941). Kurosawa was responsible for the second unit photography and spent one whole year on location. *Horses* starred Hideko Takamine and in later years when Kurosawa had gained renown as a director, there were speculations about a romance between the two at that time.

During this period Kurosawa published his first screenplay, *The Daruma Temple* (1941). His second effort, *All is Quiet* (1942), won the Nihon Eiga contest for the best scenario and a prize awarded by the Education Minister. It was not filmed, however, because it failed to meet the government's war-time priorities.

In 1943, after seven years of apprenticeship, Kurosawa finally achieved the rank of full director. For his debut he chose a new novel by Tsuneo Tomita, partly because of the restrictions imposed by the military government and partly because the subject suited him. His instincts were correct and with the release of *Sanshiro Sugata* (1943), Kurosawa achieved immediate recognition. The film was not, however, a complete critical success (some reviewers found the work saddled with too many hidden implications), but it certainly marked him as a force to be watched. Beginning a tradition which was to follow for the rest of his career, Kurosawa wrote his own scenario. He continued to script or co-script every film, except for *Those Who Make Tomorrow* (1946). The cast of *Sanshiro Sugata* included Susumu Fujita, who later appeared in *The Men Who Tread on the Tiger's Tail* (1945) and *The Hidden Fortress* (1958), and Takashi Shimura who subsequently starred in *Drunken Angel* (1948) and *Ikiru* (1952). Kurosawa has tended to work with a small repertory group of actors, using the same people over and over again. Of this group Shimura and Toshiro Mifune are the most stable members, Shimura appearing in 21 films, Mifune in 16.

Kurosawa's second feature, *The Most Beautiful* (1944) had a contemporary setting with a cast almost exclusively female. Not noted for his treatment of women (Kurosawa has admitted that his female characters are all rather strange), they would be central figures in only two more films — *No Regrets for Our Youth* (1946) and *Rashomon* (1950). It was rumored that Kurosawa was in love with his star, and soon afterwards he married Yoko Yaguchi, the actress in the cast. The two were married on February 15, 1945, and later had two children: a son Hisao, born December 20, 1945, and a daughter Kazuko, born January 29, 1954.

Because of the success of *Sanshiro Sugata*, Toho Studios decided to make a sequel in 1945. Despite poor critical reviews, the sequel, like the first version, drew large crowds of people eager to be entertained and to forget wartime realities. For Kurosawa, however, "This film did not interest me in the slightest. I had already done it once before."[2]

Kurosawa's last wartime film was an adaptation of the famous Kabuki play, *Kanjincho*. Kurosawa had wanted to make a costume drama, the choice of acceptable subjects being limited during the war, but when the first project fell through, he made *The Men Who Tread on the Tiger's Tail* instead. The completed film was not released, however. At first considered too liberal by the military regime, and then too feudalistic by the American Occupation forces, it was banned until 1952. The two parts of *Sanshiro Sugata* were also banned by the American Occupation forces. When the film was finally shown, it met with moderate favor, appearing an anomaly in light of Kurosawa's later works. In America, the film was not seen until 1960, following on the heels of his better known works. Received coolly, the film struck most critics as esoteric and alien and few felt qualified to form intelligent judgments.

During 1946 Kurosawa worked on a cooperative venture with Kajiro Yamamoto and Hideo Sekigawa. Together they made *Those Who Make Tomorrow,* a socialist propaganda film, for the labor union. The film was neither successful critically nor commercially. Reviewers found the work pseudo-ideological and overly sentimental. Kurosawa has virtually disclaimed it as a part of his work, having spent only one week actually filming. He evaluated the project as follows, '[It] is an excellent example of why a committee-made film is no good."[3]

Kurosawa's next project was *No Regrets for Our Youth* (1946). Although not considered a masterpiece, the critics felt it was one of the best early postwar films to be made in Japan. Loosely based on the government's suppression of Communist agitators at Kyoto University in 1933, the film reflected some of Kurosawa's earlier Marxist thinking. It placed number two on the *Kinema Jumpo* list of the ten best films of the year (voted on by the journal critics) and thus earned Kurosawa his first major recognition.

During 1946 Kurosawa also directed *One Wonderful Sunday* (1947) which pictured the hardships of the postwar period. The film received good critical response and placed number six on the *Kinema Jumpo* list. This film, plus *No*

Regrets for Our Youth, gained Kurosawa the best director award for 1947 granted by *Mainichi*, a leading Tokyo newspaper. Despite the recognition, Kurosawa has commented that *One Wonderful Sunday* "is certainly by no means my favourite picture."[4]

With his next film, *Drunken Angel* (1948), the story of a washed-up, petty gangster who discovers he has tuberculosis and the slum doctor who wants to cure him, Kurosawa felt "I finally discovered myself."[5] The critics agreed and for many years the film was considered Kurosawa's most important work. Placing first in the *Kinema Jumpo* listing, the film was also named Best Picture of the Year by *Mainichi* and received a prize from the Ministry of Education.

Kurosawa attributed much of the success of *Drunken Angel* to his complete autonomy during production and to the vitality and influence of Toshiro Mifune. This was Mifune's first film with Kurosawa. The two were to collaborate together for the next twenty years, their last film being *Red Beard* (1965).

Another important factor in the film's success was the contribution of Fumio Hayasaka who composed the score. Beginning with *Drunken Angel* (1948) Hayasaka scored all but one of Kurosawa's films until his death shortly after *Seven Samurai* (1954). More than a composer, Hayasaka also thought up story ideas and helped with scripting. *Drunken Angel* was extremely popular in Japan and established Kurosawa as one of the country's foremost directors. Although the work highlighted the dreariness of postwar Tokyo, its attention to psychological insights prompted audience response. The film did not reach the United States until 1959, but received consistently good reviews here.

Preceding the film's release, the Toho workers went on a 200-day strike. During this turbulent period Kurosawa, Yamamoto and a group of other artists left Toho to organize the Motion Picture Artists Association (Eiga Geijutsuka Kyokai). For his first work with this independent producing group Kurosawa chose a popular, modern Japanese drama which offered a new challenge for Mifune. He also selected the work because it seemed manageable given the limitations of a young production unit. The film, *The Quiet Duel* (1949), took seventh place on the *Kinema Jumpo* list, but did not make a big stir.

Kurosawa's next film, *Stray Dog* (1949), won wide acclaim. But Kurosawa has commented, "Everyone liked the picture, but I do not. It is too *technical* — all that technique and I had not one real thought in it."[6] Kurosawa launched the project because of his fondness for George Simenon. First he wrote an original novel in the Simenon manner, then he and Ryuzo Kikushima adapted it for the screen. The story was based on a real incident about a young policeman who loses his pistol. The film placed number three on the *Kinema Jumpo* list and first place in the *Eiga Geijutsu* (Motion Picture Art Magazine) contest. It also received an award from the Ministry of Education. In America when the film was released in 1964, it drew divided reaction. Several critics praised Kurosawa's humanity and his strong sense of visual style, while others found the work crude and uneven.

Scandal (1950), Kurosawa's next film, was his first work for the Shochiku Motion Picture Company. According to Kurosawa the movie was clearly a protest film "connected with the rise of the press in Japan."[7] The film depicts the exploitative nature of the media, a major factor in Kurosawa's refusal to grant personal interviews.

Kurosawa's next film, *Rashomon* (1950), is probably his most acclaimed and popular work. The film was also responsible for making his name known throughout the world and for alerting Western critics and viewers to the riches of the Japanese cinema.

Rashomon, an experiment in cinematic narration, was made for Daiei Motion Picture Company which was perplexed by Kurosawa's innovations and generally displeased by the results. The Japanese public was equally unmoved and the film managed only to earn back its production costs when first released. It placed number five on the *Kinema Jumpo* list, but did earn the Tokyo Motion Picture Reviewers' Club Blue Ribbon Award for the best Japaness screenplay.

However, Guiliana Stramigioli, head of Unitalia Film, saw the work and was impressed by its strength and freshness. She convinced Daiei to submit it to the Venice Film Festival in 1951 and it took the film community by surprise, walking off with the Grand Prize. Subsequently it had a glorious reception in Europe and the United States (with only a few dissenting voices). Winning an Academy Award as the best foreign film for 1951 and awards from the New York Film Critics' Group and the National Board of Review, it subsequently returned to Japan where it was acclaimed as a great film. When it opened in New York in 1951 it was the first Japanese film to play commercially in fourteen years.

The success of *Rashomon* in America led to continuing interest in Kurosawa and eventually many of his earlier works were shown commercially, especially during the early sixties.

Before all this glory, Kurosawa suffered one of the greatest disappointments of his career. For years he had loved and admired the works of Dostoyevsky and following *Rashomon* he filmed *The Idiot* (1951). For Kurosawa this was a labor of love. Unhappily, critics were unanimous in their adverse reactions. Kurosawa has commented that it was one of his most difficult projects, and that despite public reaction, he does not consider the work a failure.

When finished, *The Idiot* ran 190 minutes, which Shochiku felt was commercially unviable, and threatened to cut it in half. To this the director replied, "If you want to cut it, you had better cut it lengthwise."[8]

The Idiot was released in 1951 and proved a commercial failure. When it was shown in the States in 1963, the response was equally poor. But Kurosawa, looking back on the project in 1964, said, "One should be brave enough to risk this kind of 'mistake.' "[9]

It was during these troubles that news of the Venice Film Festival Award for *Rashomon* arrived. It pulled Kurosawa out of his despondency. On receiving the prize he commented, "I feel very happy. I would have been happier, however, if I had won the prize [with] a film depicting the reality of contemporary Japanese society."[10]

Daiei was, of course, delighted and gave a large reception. Kurosawa, however, registered his indignation at their original handling of the film by not attending the party.

Now at the height of his career, Kurosawa embarked on a period which was to see the creation of one masterpiece after another. *Ikiru* (1952) was immediately hailed in Japan as a major work and received solid critical acclaim. It placed number one in the *Kinema Jumpo* list, received a prize from the Ministry of Education and was named best picture and best screenplay in the *Mainichi Shimbun* Film Contest.

Kurosawa has commented that the genesis of the film was motivated by his own musings about death. For *Ikiru*, Kurosawa returned to Toho where he remained until 1960. When *Ikiru* was shown in America the film was recognized as a monumental work, although most of the critics cited individual flaws. In 1961 the film was honored with the David O. Selznick "Golden Laurel" Award.

Seven Samurai (1954), Kurosawa's next film was one of the director's most difficult projects and took an entire year to film. It turned out to be a studio headache and Toho's most expensive production to date. When released, it won immediate critical praise, although some resisted its three hour length. The film was subsequently shortened. When shown in America in 1956, it was hailed as a masterpiece. It placed number three on the *Kinema Jumpo* list and received a "Silver Lion" at the Venice Film Festival.

During the filming of *Seven Samurai*, Kurosawa's good friend Hayasaka was living out his last days in the hospital. They discussed dying and its effect on work, and these discussions led to the making of *Record of a Living Being* (1955). Originally they favored a satire on something like the H-bomb, but gradually Kurosawa found that satire didn't work. Kurosawa has admitted that the film seems incoherent and chaotic. It turned out to be one of his biggest box-office failures, although the reviews were good. It placed number four in the *Kinema Jumpo* list and number eight in the Tokyo Movie Reviewers' list. In the United States, where it was shown in 1967, it received mixed reactions and was written off as a minor work by a major director. Just as filming was almost complete, Hayasaka died. His death affected Kurosawa very deeply, leaving him with barely enough strength to finish the film.

Kurosawa had long desired to make a film version of *Macbeth*. After *Record of a Living Being* (1955), he set about writing a screenplay. He was intending only to produce the film, but when Toho realized the expense of the project, they assigned Kurosawa to direct. *The Throne of Blood* (1957) proved to be another difficult production with lengthy location shooting, this time on Mt. Fuji. The film, conceived in the Noh style, was an experiment like *Rashomon* (1950). This time, however, the Japanese press was more receptive.

"I've always thought that the Japanese jidai film is historically uninformed. Also, it never uses modern film-making techniques. In *Seven Samurai* (1954) we tried to do something about this, and *The Throne of Blood* had the same general feeling behind it."[11] *The Throne of Blood* placed number four in the *Kinema Jumpo* list and was well received at the Venice Film Festival. In 1961 the American critics were divided, reactions varying from one extreme to another. Some critics found the work very mannered, while others believed it was the finest adaptation of Shakespeare ever filmed.

The Lower Depths (1957), was the fulfillment of yet another long-cherished dream — to bring the work of Maxim Gorky to the screen. This time, however, the filming went smoothly. Kurosawa tried a new technique. Assembling all his actors in full costume, on the single set, he rehearsed the ensemble for forty days before turning on the cameras. The film was a qualified success and placed number ten in the *Kinema Jumpo* list. The U.S. response in 1962 was also reserved.

In October, 1957, Kurosawa travelled to England for the opening of the new National Film Theatre. There, he was honored along with other film directors like John Ford, René Clair and Vittorio de Sica. This occasion provided an opportunity to meet and talk with Ford, the director he considers the greatest influence on his own work. Other favorites are Abel Gance (the first director who really impressed Kurosawa), George Stevens and Howard Hawks, whose films he saw as a child, Frank Capra, William Wyler, Michelangelo Antonioni and Roberto Rossellini. Of the Japanese directors, he favors Kenji Mizoguchi and Keisuke Kinoshita because he considers them "purely Japanese."

Back in Japan Kurosawa began work on *The Hidden Fortress* (1958), a fairy tale story dealing with a disguised princess, her loyal general, and a treasure of hidden gold. Again weather conditions during location shooting proved problematic. But the film was a great success. The picture won the NHK Network award, a Blue Ribbon Prize, and placed number two on the *Kinema Jumpo* list. Kurosawa was also given a Golden Bear Award for best director at the Berlin Film Festival in 1959. The film was very popular in the States as well. Critics found the work highly entertaining, if somewhat superficial when it was shown in 1962.

On January 29, 1959, Kurosawa gave his first press interview. During this session he announced the formation of Kurosawa Productions, an independent producing company, to be financed with ¥ 1,000,000 by Toho. Their two year contract called for three films and specified that Kurosawa would share equally in the company's profits and losses. Kurosawa Productions became the first independent film company in the history of Japan to be headed by a working director. Production began on February 1, 1959. Now in truth, Kurosawa was the tenno (emperor) that the press had always called him.

For his first film Kurosawa chose *The Bad Sleep Well* (1960). The story concerns cooperative corruption and one man's attempt at revenge. Like his first film for The Motion Picture Artists' Association, he chose a social theme with little concern as to whether it would be financially successful. As it turned out the film placed number three on the *Kinema Jumpo* list, but received rather poor reviews in the United States three years later.

But Kurosawa's next film *Yojimbo* (1961), more than compensated for any losses on *The Bad Sleep Well*. Kurosawa was taken with the idea of filming the bad' against 'the bad' and wondered if it had ever been done before. *Yojimbo* proved to be Kurosawa's biggest box-office success and placed number two in the *Kinema Jumpo* list. The following year it reached the States and earned consistently good reviews from critics, who all noted its connection with the Hollywood Western.

Before *Yojimbo* Kurosawa had written a script about Sanjuro, a mediocre masterless samurai. After the success of *Yojimbo*, the script had to be rewritten to create a more appealing hero. Kurosawa toyed with the notion of including a color sequence, but finally rejected the idea. Later he inserted a color sequence in *High and Low* (1963). *Sanjuro* (1962) was, like its predecessor, a big hit. Comparing reactions to the two films, Kurosawa said, "I think it very different from *Yojimbo* — in Japan the audiences do too. The youngsters loved *Yojimbo*, but it was the adults who liked *Sanjuro*. I think they liked it because it was the funnier and really the more attractive of the two films."[12] The film placed number five on the *Kinema Jumpo* list. In America *Sanjuro* received mixed reviews.

Next Kurosawa directed *High and Low* (1963), another detective story like *Stray Dog*. Of the two, Kurosawa preferred the earlier film. *High and Low* was listed number two in the *Kinema Jumpo* ratings and was awarded best screenplay and best picture by *Mainichi*. In the United States it also earned praiseworthy comments.

Kurosawa's last production for Kurosawa Productions and his last film with Mifune was *Red Beard*. Commenting on the origins of the film, Kurosawa stated, "I had something special in mind when I made this film [he even issued a public statement that in it he 'wanted to push the confines of movie-making to their limits....'] because I wanted to make something that my audience would *want* to see it, something so magnificent that people would just have to see it. To do this we all worked harder than ever, tried to overlook no detail, were willing to undergo any hardship. It was really hard work [and the film took longer before the cameras than any other Japanese film including *Seven Samurai* — almost two years] and I got sick twice. Mifune and Kayama each got sick once...."[13] Although the Japanese treated it as a masterpiece, the U.S. response three years later was reserved. Many saw it as overly sentimental. In Japan it placed first on the *Kinema Jumpo* list, was named Best Picture of the Year by *Mainichi* and won a Blue Ribbon Award. That same year Kurosawa was given the Ramon Magsaysav Memorial Award in literature and journalism in Manila.

Beginning in 1966, Hollywood producer Joseph E. Levine began to woo Kurosawa. Hoping to find greater artistic freedom in the West, he signed a contract in July, 1966, to make his first color film to be called *The Runaway Train*. Together with Mifune he moved to America. The film, alternatively titled *The Mad Locomotive* and *The Longest Ride*, was never realized. Kurosawa insisted on expensive location shooting and eventually the project was dropped.

Kurosawa's next American project was 20th Century-Fox's *Tora! Tora! Tora!*, a U.S.-Japanese spectacular chronicling the events leading up to the bombing of Pearl Harbor. Kurosawa was to direct the Japanese sequences. Again disagreements ensued and on December 25, 1968, the newspapers reported that Kurosawa would be relieved of his duties because of illness. The film, directed by Richard Fleischer (Japanese sequences by Toshio Masuda), was released in 1970.

Disillusioned with filmmaking in America, Kurosawa returned to Japan. But the situation in Japan was little better. In a statement to *Variety*, published in February, 1971, he decried the state of the Japanese film industry and stated his belief in independent production as the only means of safeguarding artistic expression.

Starting again, Kurosawa formed *Yonki no Kai*, a producing company, with directors Keisuke Kinoshita, Kon Ichikawa, and Masaki Kobayashi. After a five year hiatus, Kurosawa completed *Dodeskaden* (1970), his first film in color. The film deals with the lower stratums of society and presents a rather pessimistic view of the human predicament. The work was well received in Japan, placing number three on the *Kinema Jumpo* list. It also won a special prize at the 7th International Film Festival in Moscow. In the United States, the reviews were reserved, but respectful, when the film was screened at the New York Film Festival.

Then on December 22, 1971, a maid found Kurosawa in a half-filled bathtub with twenty-two slashes on his neck, elbow, wrists, and hands. Despondent over his career and the commercial failure of *Dodeskaden*, he had tried to take his own life. Kurosawa was sixty-one at the time.

Recovering from the attempted suicide, Kurosawa was invited by the Russians to direct a co-production. For the next four years he prepared the project. The result was *Dersu Uzala* (1975), based on a story about a Russian ethnographer which had fascinated Kurosawa for thirty years. Filmed in Siberia in 70mm under rigorous weather conditions, the actual production took two years. During this period Kurosawa suffered a leg ailment as a result of the sub-zero temperatures. *Dersu Uzala* placed number five on the *Kinema Jumpo* list and won an Academy Award in 1975, although it had not been released commercially. It was, however, widely seen in Russia. In addition, it won a Gold Medal at the 9th International Film Festival in Moscow and an award from the Federation of International Film Critics.

In 1976 Kurosawa became involved in yet another fight over the editing of his films. Angered by Sovexport's decision to cut twenty minutes of the Italian release print of *Dersu Uzala* without his permission and to add different music, he threatened never to work with the Russians again. Conceding to the director's demands, Sovexport backed down.

The same year Kurosawa received a major honor from the Japanese government. Appointed a *Person of Cultural Merits,* he was the first member of the film profession to be so honored.

As of this writing no film is in production, although Kurosawa has developed several projects. Speaking out again in November, 1976, Kurosawa attacked the commercialism which dominates the Japanese scene and lamented the impossibility of working in Japan. He has again given thought to working in other countries.

At sixty-eight Kurosawa is balding, but his tall, lean body, typically un-Japanese, is still impressive. He spends his leisure time fishing, his favorite pastime next to filming. Honored as Japan's sole-living master, the critic Akira Iwasaki has summed up his career as follows: "The thing which distinguishes Kurosawa Akira from other Japanese directors — I would go so far as to call it his great achievement — is precisely that he is first and foremost a director of ideas."[14] Commenting on his ideas and their relationship to his filmmaking, Kurosawa summarized his career as follows, "The director really always makes his film for himself.... If he says he makes it for the public, he is really lying. If the film is liked by the public and seems made for them, this is because their ideas are the same as the director's and not the other way around."[15] In the end, Kurosawa's work is an extension of the man.

NOTES

1. Joan Mellen, *Voices From the Japanese Cinema* (New York: Liveright, 1975), pp. 44-45.
2. Donald Richie, "Kurosawa on Kurosawa," *Sight and Sound,* vol. 33, no. 3, Summer, 1964, p. 109.
3. *Ibid.*
4. *Ibid.,* p. 110.
5. *Ibid.*
6. *Ibid.,* p. 111.
7. *Ibid.*
8. *Ibid.,* p. 113.
9. *Ibid.*
10. "Akira Kurosawa: World Famed Film Director," *Profiles,* 1959, p. 52.
11. Donald Richie, *The Films of Akira Kurosawa* (Berkeley: University of California Press, 1970), p. 115.
12. Richie, "Kurosawa on Kurosawa," *Sight and Sound,* vol. 33, no. 4, Autumn, 1964, p. 203.
13. Richie, *The Films of Akira Kurosawa,* p. 171.
14. Akira Iwasaki, "Kurosawa and His Work," *Japan Quarterly,* vol. 12, no. 1, January-March, 1965, p. 61.
15. Richie, *The Films of Akira Kurosawa,* p. 198.

Critical Survey of Oeuvre

THEMES

Nature of Good and Evil

From the first Kurosawa has devoted considerable attention to exploring the nature of good and evil. In one form or another this question arises in all of his films. The nature of evil can be the individual acts (murder, rape or kidnapping) of a criminal as in *Stray Dog, Rashomon, The Throne of Blood, Sanjuro* and *High and Low*; a corruptive group within a society as in *No Regrets for Our Youth, Scandal, Seven Samurai, The Hidden Fortress, The Bad Sleep Well* and *Yojimbo*; or the human predicament itself with its incumbent miseries. Human suffering, a form of evil, is portrayed by Kurosawa in *The Most Beautiful, One Wonderful Sunday, Drunken Angel, The Idiot, Record of a Living Being, The Lower Depths, Dodeskaden*, and most eloquently in *Ikiru*.

Kurosawa has directed two crime films (*Stray Dog* and *High and Low*). Based on the classic formula, he juxtaposes the detective/hero against the criminal, while the main body of the work is given over to catching the villain. However, as opposed to many films in this genre, the villain is exposed early and we are given an opportunity to come to know the criminal and his world as a means of better understanding the nature of evil.

Despite Kurosawa's quest for knowledge, there never exists any doubt concerning the need to punish evil and the necessity for the hero to take action. In both films Kurosawa reveals the close link which binds the hero to the villain and visually unites the two in one image (the two men indistinguishable and covered with mud in *Stray Dog*, the image of two figures superimposed on the glass partition in *High and Low*). Both are part of one world, and how one lives does affect the other. By showing similarities, Kurosawa emphasizes the importance of choice and individual action. In other words, given identical circumstances, one man choses one path; a second man, another. We are what we do. In sentiments close to existential philosophic thought, Kurosawa posits each man's ultimate responsibility for himself. This idea is the notion that corruption is a form of weakness, an idea fully realized in Kurosawa's depiction of Hiruta in *Scandal*. Charles Higham has stated, "He [Kurosawa] deals with the most primitive human emotions: greed, fear, lust, the desire to kill and hunt.... He is concerned with the reasons for man's unhappiness in the world and with man's tragic repetition of his past mistakes, but he does not attempt facile solutions."[1]

Kurosawa's crime films devote considerable footage to the process of detection in a manner similar to Fritz Lang's *M*. In many respects these passages are miniature documentaries. The rendering of the identification division and the ballistics laboratory in *Stray Dog* and the close attention to police procedures in *High and Low* demonstrate Kurosawa's interest in technical processes. This fascination shows up again in the detailing of surgical procedures in *The Quiet Duel* and *Red Beard*, in the lengthy court hearings in *Scandal*, and in the depiction of bureaucratic red tape in *Ikiru*.

Another aspect of Kurosawa's treatment of evil relates to the corruptive nature of power. This forms the central theme in *The Throne of Blood*. Unlike Shakespeare's Macbeth, who is motivated by blinding ambition, as Richie has pointed out, Washizu's "fault" is his failure to realize himself completely. Washizu reacts weakly to the forces which surround him, rather than taking the initiative like Macbeth. "Naturally, one murder leads to the other, because this is the pattern of power."[2]

The Bad Sleep Well reveals further reflections on the nature of power. Nishi, in his efforts to avenge his father's death, finally adopts tactics identical to those used by the corrupt capitalists. Although the failure to accomplish his mission is complicated by several factors, the implicit message of the film rests on the power of evil to contaminate us all.

Kurosawa first treated the subject of large scale corruption and crime in *Scandal*, a film which deals with press exploitation and the invasion of privacy. This theme reappears in *Seven Samurai* as the hostile brigands attack the defenseless farmers. It is developed more fully in *Drunken Angel*, which depicts the petty criminals who inhabit the underworld and again in *The Bad Sleep Well* where unseen powers control individual destinies and infect all of society. In a similar way, *Record of a Living Being* calls into question the degree to which governments rule in the people's interest or whether in subtle ways they are not as harmful as Washizu's tyranny.

Lastly, Kurosawa focuses on the evils of disease, ignorance, poverty, war and ultimately death. These become central issues in his treatment of postwar conditions in *One Wonderful Sunday*. He deals with the effect of venereal disease in *The Quiet Duel*, tuberculosis in *Drunken Angel* and *Scandal*, the solitude and pain of death in *Red Beard* and *Ikiru*, and the overwhelming desolation of the poor in *The Lower Depths* and *Dodeskaden*. On occasion disease becomes a symbolic manifestation of inner corruption as in *Drunken Angel* or the failure to live a meaningful life as in *Ikiru*. Dying also provides the protagonist with a heightened perception as in these two films or in *Scandal*. But generally disease, death and poverty are treated as part of the human predicament to be suffered and endured.

As in his treatment of social and political evil, Kurosawa often raises problems, but does not always provide solutions. The worlds portrayed in *The Lower Depths* and *Dodeskaden* are closed and no action is possible other than death and dreaming. Little attempt is made to relate dramatized conditions to economic factors or to present possibilities for remedy. Causes are implied, but not treated in depth. Marty Gliserman criticized *Dodeskaden* and Kurosawa's failure to confront this issue, stating "To live in such a way that one has only dreams, fantasies and delusions as a means of escaping or dealing with intolerable realities is psychologically destructive and politically regressive."[3] On the other hand, Joan Mellen, treating the identical theme concluded that "the imagined is made morally superior to the unmediated real because it bears with it the felt experience of the individual.... These become symbolic of man's transcendent imagination and of his intrinsic value as a creature whose magical fantasies and ability to survive become miracles of their own."[4]

A final word should be added about *Rashomon*. Clearly Kurosawa is commenting on the universality of evil and the potential of all men for criminal action. However, this does not automatically imply that Kurosawa holds a pessimistic view of mankind. The act of kindness which closes the film (the adoption of the baby) certainly reveals man's capacity for good, as well as for evil.

The Kurosawa Hero

Most Kurosawa films have a clearly defined hero at the center of the action. In one way or another these men (in one or two cases women) have set themselves the task of combating evil in the forms previously discussed.

The men themselves are not paragons of virtue, but rather humans in the process of moral and philosophic development. (The samurai films differ slightly and will be treated separately below.) Often the hero is a young man influenced by an older male who serves as his mentor. *Sanshiro Sugata* is exemplary in its establishment of the relationship between the young Sugata and the older judo master. Shimura plays the role of mentor in *Stray Dog* and *Seven Samurai* and Mifune assumes the mantle later in *Red Beard*.

In addition to the struggle against outer evil forces, Kurosawa films focus upon the struggle within, the hero's efforts to come to terms with himself. The evolution of the hero sets him apart from the villain, who is completely formed and thus spiritually stifled. Often the hero fights against his own pride as in *Sanshiro Sugata* and *Red Beard*. Matsunaga in *Drunken Angel* and Washizu in *The Throne of Blood* confront the same human frailty, but less successfully. In all cases, the films represent a quest for self-knowledge. Along the way the hero undergoes a test. The test can take various forms, but usually requires some kind of sacrifice or suffering, which ultimately will redeem him. This emphasis on sacrifice and suffering constitutes one of the aspects of Kurosawa's work which has prompted critics to call his films Dostoyevskian. The challenges confronted by particular heroes and heroines include: Yukie's commitment to her political beliefs and the sacrifice of a comfortable life in *No Regrets for Our Youth;* Fujisaki's painful battle against venereal disease and the end of his engagement in *The Quiet Duel;* and Yasumoto's internship at the Koishikawa Public clinic and his ultimate decision to forego a career in the Shogun's service.

In other films the challenge is not so clearly a question of sacrifice, but of commitment to society. Sanada's determination to practice medicine among the poor in *Drunken Angel;* the seven samurai's acceptance of menial rewards for protecting the farmers; Red Beard's devotion to his medical practice and Harada's volunteer work as a judge in *Record of a Living Being,* all represent responsible action.

Kurosawa's films clearly posit man's responsibility to society and to other men. This is one aspect of his humanism. Small details pervade all of the films and emphasize the extent to which our lives are interdependent. In *The Bad Sleep Well,* Tatsuo publicly states his responsibility for his sister's happiness. in *Stray Dog,* Sato feels accountable to the millions of ordinary citizens who could become innocent victims. In *Red Beard,* Niide demands that all physicians at the clinic share their knowledge for the benefit of mankind. The concern of Sato and Niide for all humanity separate them from Murakami and Yasumoto whose professional actions are motivated by personal concerns, guilt and embarrassment in the case of Murakami; pride and concern for reputation in the case of Yasumoto. Kurosawa further posits man's obligation to preserve his own life, to stay alive, again an existential concept. In *Dodeskaden,* Tanba convinces his neighbor of life's basic worth and of his responsibility for keeping alive the memory of those he has loved.

Perhaps the most explicit statements of man's debt towards others are the samurai's willingness to aid the defenseless village and Gondo's decision in *High and Low* to ransom the chauffeur's son. In both films the heroes commit themselves to causes not rightfully their own and suffer extreme consequences. But these men, once presented with a choice, must adopt a moral stance if they are to be heroes.

Failure to recognize one's responsibility to others leads to death and destruction. When Kikuchiyo leaves his post in *Seven Samurai,* he endangers the lives of everyone and causes the death of several villagers. Likewise, when the police initially opt not to arrest Takeuchi in *High and Low,* this leads to the death of an innocent prostitute. Like Murakami and Yasumoto, these men are acting on selfish motives. Ultimately the desire for personal action must be balanced against the greater good. In many ways this notion reflects the traditional Japanese struggle between giri (desire) and ninjo (duty).

The heroes of Kurosawa's films are often solitary men who live alone in this world, unattached to family and friends. This is especially true of the samurai heroes in *Yojimbo, Sanjuro* and *Seven Samurai.* In no case do these men integrate themselves permanently into the community, but rather, like the archetypal cowboy, ride off into the sunset once their mission is accomplished. But the hero's isolation is equally characteristic of Niide in *Red Beard*, Sanada in *Drunken Angel* and other protagonists. Their detachment from the life of ordinary men allows them time to develop spiritually and to devote themselves with full commitment.

In fact, it might be stated that Kurosawa's failed heroes, men like Nishi in *The Bad Sleep Well* and Nakajima in *Record of a Living Being* are undone as much by personal entanglements as by the enormous odds against which they fight. Unlike the more successful heroes, Nishi and Nakajima lack the dispassionate objectivity which comes from living a life apart and are flawed men — ruled by passion and obsession, rather than by logic.

The samurai heroes are more fully formed than Kurosawa's contemporary men. At least, we happen in on them after they have completed the process of their education. In the main they exhibit the kind of moral rectitude we have come to expect from a Kurosawa hero. However, as opposed to the contemporary heroes who are all ordinary men, the samurai are characterized by superhuman qualities which are almost mythic. They are men of high energy, sharp intelligence, and flawless skill. They seldom make a mistake. These attributes link them with all other samurai within the genre. It is Kurosawa's ability to humanize these men, despite their disproportionate advantages, that differentiate them from the heroes of other directors.

Reality vs. Illusion

Throughout his book, *The Films of Akira Kurosawa*, Donald Richie discusses the director's continual preoccupation with the discrepancy between illusion and reality. This theme takes various forms: on a simple level it deals with the masks men wear and the difficulty of ascertaining truth about other men; on a second level it deals with the discrepancy between man's dreams and the reality of his world, and the ways in which man deludes himself; and lastly it touches upon the multiple facets of reality and the impossibility of knowing truth.

Disguises are an important element in many Kurosawa films. In some cases characters simply conceal motives, in others they assume a complete change of identity. In *No Regrets for Our Youth*, Noge conceals his true commitment to the Communist cause, as in *Scandal*, Hiruta fails to reveal his duplicity until the end. Changes of identity occur in *The Men Who Tread on the Tiger's Tail*, *Stray Dog*, and *The Hidden Fortress* and pervade *Seven Samurai* (Kambei disguises himself as a priest; Kikuchiyo, a farmer's son, poses as a samurai; later he dresses as a brigand; and Shino dresses as a boy). Perhaps the culmination of this theme occurs in *The Bad Sleep Well*. Here, almost all of the characters wear masks of respectability, though inwardly they remain corrupt. It seems appropriate, therefore, that Nishi also adopt a false identity in order to unmask them. In *Sanjuro*, Tsubaki states this theme perfectly when he warns the young samurai that men are seldom what they seem.

In *One Wonderful Sunday,* Kurosawa presents viewers with the sounds of an orchestra, clearly the wish fulfillment of the two lovers. These sounds, like the clanking of the trolley years later in *Dodeskaden,* or the dream mansions of the father and son, or Miki's ghost in *The Throne of Blood* represent the subjective reality of the characters, their dreams and nightmares. In other Kurosawa films, man's dreams and illusions are not depicted in such concrete form, but arise from dialogue and action.

Man's capability for self-deception becomes a central concern in *Rashomon.* Though each character accepts responsibility for the husband's murder, each arranges the truth to reflect most admirably on himself or herself and on those personality characteristics which he or she holds most dear.

The Lower Depths provides a fine example of how man feeds on dreams and self-deception to make life bearable. Osen, the whore, talks of great loves which may or may not have been; the ex-samurai revels in stories of past exploits; and Tomekichi, the tinker, continues to think of himself as a craftsman though he no longer works. Poignancy and human sympathy arise here, as in *One Wonderful Sunday* and *Dodeskaden,* from the gap between truth and reality, dream and possibility.

The difficulty of finding truth and the multiple levels of reality arise in Kurosawa's first film, *Sanshiro Sugata.* In searching for strength Sugata develops his physical prowess only to learn that true strength comes from the perfection of the spirit.

The elusive quality of truth is best depicted, of course, in *Rashomon,* a film which presents four versions of the same event, all with contradictory evidence. Many critics have unsuccessfully attempted to reconcile the various stories into one version of reality. But to unravel the puzzle is to miss the point. The message lies specifically in the multiplicity of truth, the fragmentary nature of the world, and man's limited capacity for understanding.

The difficulty of separating illusion from reality is a central theme of *Record of a Living Being.* The inability to reconcile his truth with the reality which surrounds him, drives Nakajima insane. Kurosawa makes no attempt to settle the question of the H-bomb. Rather, the issue, like the murder in *Rashomon,* remains unresolved.

Few people have the capacity to confront truth directly. Either they sink into despair or become cynical like the priest in *The Lower Depths.* Those with moral convictions, like Red Beard, accept the limitations of man and redouble their commitment to humanity. For the rest, they turn to dreams and self-deception like the characters in *The Lower Depths* and *Dodeskaden.* No film better illustrates how men distort truth than *Ikiru,* where we witness the contagious nature of self-deception during the progress of the funeral scene.

A minor variation on the theme of reality relates to the film medium itself as the purveyor of illusions. One would hardly expect Kurosawa to ignore this rich possibility. In the courtroom scene in *Scandal,* Kurosawa films Hiruta's entrance, immediately followed by a repetition of the same action in the movie newsreel. Clearly this passage indicates the difference between physical reality and film reality. More blatant, Kurosawa demonstrates in *Scandal* how photography can be manipulated to create false realities. Alternatively, in *The Bad Sleep Well*, the tape recording reveals a truth hidden by the events themselves. In this case, the media provides an alternate truth, a corrective to the illusion.

Humor

Despite the harsh realities depicted throughout Kurosawa's work, there is scarcely a film which does not contain a comic character or several comic scenes. Sometimes it is the hero himself who is put through the comic paces; for Western audiences, this may seem like a lapse in taste or character inconsistency. When Sugata rubs his head before the big fight or Red Beard takes on a gang of thugs, the comic effects may result in a diminution of their dignity, but at the same time these actions tend to humanize them.

In *The Men Who Tread on the Tiger's Tail*, Kurosawa specifically added the porter to the traditional Kabuki drama, and cast Kenichi Enomoto, a popular comedian in the role. This alteration in the standard text created a great stir and was perceived by the Japanese censors as ridicule of traditional values. Again in *The Lower Depths* Kurosawa cast a well-known comedian in an important role. By choosing Bokuzen Hidari to play the priest and closing the film with a raucous musical performance, Kurosawa not only reaffirmed life, but also showed the mixture of comedy and tragedy which typifies the human predicament.

In Kurosawa's work, humor usually arises from ignorance or a discrepancy between the way characters see themselves and their world and our view of them. Thus humor provides a perspective on events which cannot be achieved in any other way. In this regard the woodcutter's tale in *Rashomon* is exemplary. But Kurosawa does not demean his comic characters. In fact, they often possess a vitality lacking in the other personae. Most often the comic characters are from the peasant or lower class, like the two farmers in *The Hidden Fortress*, Kikuchiyo in *Seven Samurai* or the wife-swappers in *Dodeskaden*. Exceptions do exist, however, like the young lords in *Sanjuro*.

The use of humor in Kurosawa films constitutes more than comic relief. Rather humor presents a positive response to life. In three cases Kurosawa has produced full-length comic films. In all these works, *The Hidden Fortress*, *Yojimbo*, and *Sanjuro*, Toshiro Mifune plays the lead. Mifune also plays the comic warrior in *Seven Samurai*, where his animal energy and mannerisms are well suited for the part.

Women

Women play a minor role in most Kurosawa films. He has admitted, "Women simply aren't my specialty."[5] In only one film, *No Regrets for Our Youth*, does a woman become a central figure faced with a moral dilemma equal to that of other male protagonists. For the most part, they are minor characters, either bar girls or ex-call girls (*Drunken Angel, Stray Dog, The*

Quiet Duel), young innocents (*Drunken Angel, Scandal, Dodeskaden*) or obedient wives (*The Bad Sleep Well, High and Low*). Miyako in *Scandal* does have a successful career, but she is never fully developed. Lady Asaji is a forceful character in *The Throne of Blood*, but always remains in a minor role. In *The Hidden Fortress*, Princess Yukimine possesses the male virtues of courage and leadership, but again, she is only a stereotype and never psychologically revealed.

Apart from *No Regrets for Our Youth*, Kurosawa comes closest to delving into the female psyche in *Rashomon* and *The Idiot*. Although none of the women are the single focus of the narrative, Masago, Taeko, and Ayako are all depicted with a degree of emotional complexity which goes well beyond stereotyping.

Throughout Kurosawa's work there are few intimate moments between men and women, and those that do exist are mostly devoid of sexual content. Perhaps the best exception is the scene in *The Bad Sleep Well* when Nishi first realizes his growing love for his wife and contemplates consumating their marriage.

Humanism

Joan Mellen in her essay "The Epic Cinema of Kurosawa" compares the director's films to nineteenth-century novels. Believing them to be "primarily moral in their outlook," she examines their world-view and exploration of the human condition. Quoting Kurosawa she states, '[I] keep saying the same thing over and over again. Why, I ask, is it that human beings cannot get along with each other? Why can't they live with each other with more good will?"[6]

Barbara Wolf reiterates a similar sentiment in "On Akira Kurosawa" holding that all Kurosawa films are moral allegories on "the human condition and the impossibility of escaping it."[7] Both authors perceive Kurosawa's continual concern for humanity. It is this aspect of his work that lends a sense of universality to his films despite the fact that the stories are grounded in Japanese history or modern Japanese culture. Akira Iwasaki expressed the same thought when he stated that all Kurosawa films boil down to one theme, "the problems of the existence of man, its meaning and its forms."[8]

It is Kurosawa's concern for all humanity that has led to his interest in outcasts (*The Lower Depths* and *Dodeskaden*) and peasants (*Seven Samurai* and *The Hidden Fortress*), as well as heroes and aristocrats (samurai films and *The Throne of Blood*).

Kurosawa characters, despite some larger-than-life samurai, are never totally good nor bad. The heroes as well as the villains are flawed. Sugata cannot resist a youthful display of his physical strength. Sanada drowns his sorrows in drink. The warriors in *Seven Samurai* all express human emotions and Red Beard is not beyond cruel comments and rash outbursts.

Likewise, unsympathetic characters always possess some redeeming quality. Iwabuchi in *The Bad Sleep Well* is a committed family man. Shima's wife in

Dodeskaden may appear shrewish to his guests, but she has stayed beside him during all their years of poverty.

Kurosawa never presents an idealized portrait of the peasants. Though they are victimized by the brigands in *Seven Samurai*, they are not above stripping dead samurai for armor or hiding food from their defenders. In *The Hidden Fortress* Kurosawa reveals the extent of their greed.

Part of Kurosawa's humanism derives from his ability to depict the inner forces which drive men and against which they struggle, and to indicate the larger world which influences their lives, but which remains always beyond their control. Kurosawa explores man's passions: lust (*Rashomon*), greed (*The Hidden Fortress*), ambition (*The Throne of Blood*), power (*The Bad Sleep Well*), and jealousy (*The Lower Depths*).

Likewise, his films situate characters in an environment exposing aspects of society which produce endless hardships and exacerbate volatile emotions: poverty (*High and Low*), disease (*Drunken Angel*), hunger (*Seven Samurai*), political corruption (*The Bad Sleep Well*), as well as alienation and bureaucracy which deaden men's souls as in *Ikiru*.

Kurosawa's films never portray an ideal world. Even in his most minor works the grim realities of life are clearly visible and suffering and death are never far from the minds of his characters. But as *Ikiru* reveals, not until we face dying, can we begin living. And ultimately it is *how* we live, not how we die, that is important.

The solutions are not simple; the moral not totally satisfying. Despite man's limitations and the social realities of his world, he must face life without illusion, develop his moral strength, commit himself to humanity and find hope and meaning in a world which often seems devoid of both. In the face of great obstacles, man must continue to do the best he can. Like Sanada, or Kambei, or Red Beard, man gains nobility through his struggles. It is this message which gives rise to the beauty and humanism which characterize the best of Kurosawa.

STYLE

From Kurosawa's first work, *Sanshiro Sugata* (1943), he has been an experimenter in style, technique, and narrative structure, and has availed himself fully of those potentials offered by an ever-increasing technology.

Although Kurosawa has simplified his film style in recent years, his major works are characterized by expressionistic techniques which utilize the entire range of stylistic possibilities. His first film *Sanshiro Sugata* is illlustrative, and serves as a model for his later works.

Filming and Editing

Sanshiro Sugata alternates between passages of highly mobile camerawork and heavily edited footage. The film begins with a pan from the sky to the street, an opening which reoccurs in many Kurosawa works. In addition to panning, Kurosawa uses several tracking and crane shots: the former is especially effective in creating tension during the night fight on the bridge, and the latter, in revealing the formal beauty of the umbrellas in the scene with Sayo. Elsewhere Kurosawa uses a swish pan to indicate Murai's subjective point of view. In later films, Kurosawa makes use of vertical tracking shots (*Ikiru* and *Dodeskaden*) and the zoom (*Scandal* and *Dodeskaden*) and serial, swish pans (*The Throne of Blood* and *The Hidden Fortress*).

Sanshiro Sugata abounds in close-ups, cut together with other shots which provide expressionistic detail. High and low angles are used throughout as well as overhead shots of Sugata's fight against Murai.

In this first film, Kurosawa experiments with several types of filmic punctuation. He uses dissolves to link various shots of Sugata's geta, thus indicating the passage of time; and a fade to bridge Sanshiro's victory over Higaki with the closing sequence on the train. The vertical and horizontal wipes, which become a hallmark of his style, appear throughout.

In addition to these techniques, Kurosawa utilizes slow motion photography in the final fight against Higaki and a freeze frame in Sugata's match with Momma. Later Kurosawa films utilize other forms of trick photography, such as superimposition (*Drunken Angel* and *Stray Dog*) and stop motion (*The Throne of Blood*).

Sanshiro Sugata also incorporates brief flashbacks which reflect Sugata's inner thoughts, most specifically the image of Momma's daughter and the lotus flower.

Beginning in the early fifties, the period of his maturity, Kurosawa's works lean heavily on two unique methods: the use of multiple cameras and long, focal-length lenses. Kurosawa first experimented with multiple cameras in *Record of a Living Being*. Thereafter, he used several cameras, usually three running simultaneously, in all of his films, although this number varies. In the train sequence in *High and Low*, a scene demanding tension and quick movement, he used nine cameras and in one segment of *Red Beard* he used five. Kurosawa has defended this technique as follows: "For one thing, the actors are very aware of three cameras looking at them, and one of the results is that unexpectedly real-looking expressions and postures appear. For another, you can get all sorts of interesting pictorial effects and compositions which would be impossible using only a single camera."[9]

Kurosawa first fully exploited the telephoto lens in *Seven Samurai*. By using long focal lengths he was able to flatten the distance between the background and the foreground and to create a shallow effect on the screen. In discussing this technique as used in *Red Beard*, he stated, "The actors like this fine, it got the camera far away from them, but that isn't why I did it this time. I did [sic] because I wanted to get that crowded, two-dimensional, slightly smoky effect that only a long-distance lens can give you."[10]

The use of the widescreen has also appealed to Kurosawa. His first scope film was *The Hidden Fortress*, released in 1958, just three years after Japan's first widescreen success, and since then all of his films have been produced in a wide format. With his latest film, *Dersu Uzala* (1975), he pushed the limits even further and filmed in 70 mm, which has enabled him to capture the beauties and terrors of nature, a thematic element in the film.

Kurosawa came very late to color. After the international success of *Gate of Hell* (1953), which launched color photography in Japan, Kurosawa continued to film in black and white until *Dodeskaden* in 1970. As late as 1964 Kurosawa commented, "In its present stage, color photography is too strong to represent properly the subdued color which is peculiarly Japanese. By strict standards even *Gate of Hell* was not truly Japanese.... Then too, the photosensitivity of color is so low, I can't close down my iris enough to capture the detail I like to get. And shooting simultaneously from several different camera positions as I like to do would make the cost of color prohibitive."[11]

When he finally produced *Dodeskaden*, he chose to explore the fantastic possibilities of color rather than its realistic qualities. Kurosawa had toyed with color earlier, however, first considering a color sequence in *Sanjuro* (the climatic scene in which the flowers float down the river from the Camellia House) and then including a passage in *High and Low* (the pink smoke produced when the bag containing the ransom money is burned).

Characteristic of Kurosawa's work is an emphasis on movement and a highly, dramatic visual style. Movement is achieved through camera movement, through the shifting of actors within the frame, and through editing. All scenes in Kurosawa films are designed, almost choreographed, by the director. He is especially famous for his fight and action sequences in such films as *Sanshiro Sugata*, *Seven Samurai*, *Yojimbo*, and *Sanjuro*. Frequently tension is created by editing together several short shots and reversing the dominant direction in each succeeding cut. Generally the breathtaking effects are achieved through a combination of all three types of movement mentioned above.

Kurosawa has devised some very long, complex camera sequences in his films, most specifically in *Seven Samurai*, *High and Low*, and *Red Beard*. However, unlike Orson Welles, whose genius is concentrated on long, uninterrupted tracking shots, Kurosawa favors several travelling shots edited together which gives the impression of one continuous movement. The woodcutter running through the forest in *Rashomon* and the students running up the mountain in *No Regrets for Our Youth* are typical of this procedure.

The later works tend towards longer takes and less editing. This results in complicated camera set-ups which place great demands upon the actors and necessitate long rehearsals. For *The Lower Depths*, the entire cast, in full costume, performed for long weeks in front of running cameras with no film, before Kurosawa was ready to finally begin. *The Lower Depths* elicits further interest because of its two-tiered set which allowed Kurosawa to direct several actions simultaneously within a single frame.

Another unique aspect of Kurosawa's filming technique relates to his fondness for shooting in chronological order, a procedure seldom used in standard production because of the high expenditure of time and money. He used this technique in *The Lower Depths* and in parts of *Red Beard* to capture a sense of time and mood and to achieve "the effect of one continuous take."

Kurosawa displays extreme care in the composition of his frames. He frequently utilizes a diagonal arrangement (one head lined up behind another in depth) and favors asymmetrical compositions. No doubt both tendencies reflect traditional Japanese aesthetics. In *The Throne of Blood* Kurosawa's mise-en-scène reflects his conscious attempt to imitate the formal compositions of the Noh Theater.

Kurosawa has also been immensely innovative in utilizing all four sides of the screen and in creating complex cinematic space. *The Hidden Fortress* makes great use of the extreme sides of the scope frame. And in *Scandal*, as well as other works, actors rise into frame from screen bottom, a movement seldom utilized in the commercial cinema.

Several methods are characteristic of Kurosawa's editing style: one is the montage sequence; the other is the wipe. Throughout his career Kurosawa has incorporated striking montage sequences into the text of his films. Basically they are used to indicate the passage of time (the change of seasons in *The Quiet Duel*, the amusement park sequence in *Stray Dog*, Kameda's courtship of Ayako in *The Idiot* and Yasumoto's recovery in *Red Beard*) or a repetitive process (the student demonstrations in *No Regrets for Our Youth*, the petition process in *Ikiru*, the testing of possible candidates in *Seven Samurai*, and the multiple arrests in *The Bad Sleep Well*). However, these sequences also create strong visual effects akin to well-composed paintings.

From *Sanshiro Sugata* through *Red Beard* Kurosawa has maintained a predilection for vertical and lateral wipes, a feature of late silent and early sound films long out of fashion when Kurosawa made his first feature. In his hands this rather antiquated stylistic feature becomes modern, tending to rupture the dramatic illusion and to bring forth the reality of filmmaking. On occasion he has experimented with this idiosyncratic method by creating wipes with moving objects (e.g. a truck in *Scandal*).

Writing and Acting

The majority of Kurosawa's films are based on preexisting texts, dramas, novels or short stories. As opposed to many prominent directors, he is not averse to using well-known, literary works. The results have received divided reactions. The films based on Shakespeare's *Macbeth* and Gorky's *The Lower Depths* were hailed as great successes, whereas that based on Dostoyevsky's *The Idiot* proved to be his worst failure. Despite the literary origins of Kurosawa's films, his creative direction and highly visual style have prevented these works from becoming mere cinematic adaptations.

Except for *Those Who Make Tomorrow*, Kurosawa has co-authored all of his scenarios or, in the case of his early works, scripted the films alone. Of the twenty-six works he has directed, however, he has used only six co-authors Eijiro Hisaita, Ryuzo Kikushima, Keinosuke Uegusa, Shinobu Hashimoto,

Hideo Oguni, and Masato Ide. Working together in various combinations, they have produced truly creative scenarios. Whereas the Hollywood method of team-writing has often resulted in mediocre works, Kurosawa defends his procedure. "I do not trust myself to write a script alone. It is that simple. I need people who can give me a perspective."[12]

In addition to the group of writers who have worked with Kurosawa over the years, there exists a group of actors who have remained with the director since the beginning of his career. People join and leave the repertory group, but always a nucleus remains. Certain actors like Takashi Shimura and Toshiro Mifune have prominent roles in almost every work.

While Kurosawa is writing or adapting the scenario, he is also casting his film. By selecting actors for certain roles in advance, he can create characters specifically suited to individual talents and then incorporate personal idiosyncrasies. To further integrate character and actor, Kurosawa writes full biographies for each major character in the scenario and insists upon calling his actors by their fictional name while on the set.

Sound

It is in the area of sound that Kurosawa has proven to be one of the most innovative directors. Beginning with the dramatic sequence on the windswept plain in *Sanshiro Sugata*, Kurosawa has been conscious of the impact of sound and music on the filmic experience. Through his long collaboration with Fumio Hayasaka (they worked on eight films together), he has forged a style which pays careful attention to naturalistic sound; draws upon artificial sound, often for symbolic purposes; and unifies the whole with the use of music.

Kurosawa's films are filled with background sounds such as street noises *(Record of a Living Being)* or voices from nature *(Scandal)* which lend a sense of verisimilitude to the work. Kurosawa also pays attention to off-screen sounds which relate the visible to the larger, unseen world. Sound is sometimes used to anticipate and bridge a succeeding scene in the way that the wind is heard on the soundtrack preceding Sugata's final battle, in part one.

Many of the most effective moments in Kurosawa's films are created by the use of heightened sound effects. Thus in *The Throne of Blood* the gong which reverberates as the fortress doors open or the sound of arrows finding their mark produce tense, dramatic reactions.

In the same way, the call of trumpets suddenly resounding in mountain caves in *The Hidden Fortress* achieves its effect though its context is totally artificial.

Occasionally Kurosawa uses sounds symbolically, for instance, the call of a crow *(The Throne of Blood)* and bells *(The Lower Depths* and *Red Beard)* both prefigure death while a clap of thunder foreshadows the rise of Fascism *(No Regrets for Our Youth)*. Sound is also an indicator of subjective states in several Kurosawa works, most specifically the strains of Schubert in *One Wonderful Sunday*, the sleigh bells in *The Idiot* and the trolley sounds in *Dodeskaden*.

Kurosawa's continued interest in the possibilities of sound can be seen in *Red Beard* and *Dersu Uzala*. The former is recorded on a four-track, stereo system; the latter on six-track, stereophonic sound equipment. This sophisticated technology enables Kurosawa to best capture the subtleties of human speech and natural sound and to modulate them freely.

Kurosawa's musical preferences are a blend of Eastern and Western melodies. Most of the compositions are based on Western origins and arranged for Western-style orchestras. (This is not unusual in Japan. Ozu, considered Japan's most Japanese director, used only Western scores in his films.) Often Kurosawa will borrow a familiar melody taken from the popular repertory. Such tunes turn up in *Ikiru* (*Happy Birthday*), *Stray Dog* (*The Anniversary Waltz*), *Scandal* (*Auld Lang Syne*), and *High and Low* (*O Sole Mio*). The list is long. In addition, many contemporary Kurosawa films incorporate American jazz, blues and Latin American rhythms into the context of the work. *Drunken Angel* and *Ikiru* are two such examples. The popular music is used to highlight the setting, to reveal some aspect of the character, or to create a specific mood such as nostalgia, loneliness, etc.

For Kurosawa music can be used to enhance the emotional quality of a scene or to stimulate a complex response by introducing musical themes which counterpoint the main drama. The first method is best exemplified by a film like *Rashomon* or *Red Beard* where the music heightens the action; creating tension in the former, and a sense of compassion in the latter. Another example occurs in *Yojimbo* and *Sanjuro* where action and music are so perfectly synchronized that Masaru Sato's score seems to punctuate Mifune's gestures producing a forceful, dramatic effect.

Counterpoint sound appears in a scene from *The Bad Sleep Well* where loud South American music, emanating from a tape recorder, plays over a funeral gathering thus creating a jarring response appropriate to the thematic content of the sequence.

Kurosawa's musical scores range from films with set pieces, like the Noh and Kabuki songs in *The Men Who Tread on the Tiger's Tail*, to full scores as in *Yojimbo*. Several films contain themes associated with individual characters. This occurs in *Seven Samurai*, *The Lower Depths* and *Yojimbo*.

Naturally, Kurosawa is equally conscious of the effect of silence and in certain scenes (Ayako's visit to Taeko in *The Idiot* and the funeral in *Ikiru*), he has eliminated all dialogue and music, thus allowing the absence of sound to dominate the mood. In *Ikiru* silence is used to simulate Watanabe's subjective sensations as he emerges from the clinic.

Atmosphere and Lighting

Kurosawa is also extremely sensitive to atmosphere and light and, as with sound, he has experimented with various degrees of shading. In an interview he referred to his fondness for extremes. Thus he delights in the contrast between the hot, sultry days depicted in *Stray Dog* and *Record of a Living Being* and the bitter arctic temperatures captured in *Dersu Uzala*.

Climatic conditions often set the tone for a film, symbolically indicating the mental attitudes of the characters or reflecting the director's theme. Thus the mist which pervades parts of *The Throne of Blood* mirrors Washizu's clouded perceptions, and the rain in *Rashomon*, which gives way to sunshine, visualizes the optimistic humanism which closes the film. Likewise, rain storms often occur after highly charged emotional moments (*Stray Dog* and *Record of a Living Being*) and serve as cathartic releases for the drama.

Kurosawa handles lighting with the same care lavished on other aspects of production. He has even had his lighting director fabricate a special device to produce additional illumination for outdoor shooting. Kurosawa films reveal the full range of lighting possibilities. He has portrayed delicate sunlight filtering through trees in *Rashomon* (an image which impressed many Western critics) and has caught the glaring lights of nighttime Tokyo in such works as *The Bad Sleep Well* and *Ikiru*.

Narrative Structure

Just as Kurosawa has been an experimenter in terms of technique, so too he has been in the forefront in devising new methods for rendering dramatic action. His most radical departures are *Rashomon* and *Ikiru*, but even in other films, Kurosawa has constantly sought to create new narrative constructs.

In both *Stray Dog* and *Ikiru* Kurosawa used a voice-over narrator to set the stage and to comment on the events. This technique was utilized again years later in *Dersu Uzala*, which chronicles Arsinev's story of Dersu.

For *High and Low* Kurosawa devised a two-part structure. The first half of the film focuses on the victim, the wealthy merchant, Gondo; the second follows the exploits of the criminal, the poverty-stricken intern, Takeuchi. The break occurs midway through the film with the return of the kidnapped boy.

In two later works Kurosawa turned his attention to multiple narratives, eliminating the focus on one character and simultaneously disregarding the star system. In *The Lower Depths* and again in *Dodeskaden*, Kurosawa portrays the human predicament through a series of diverse situations and characters. In *Dodeskaden* he skillfully cuts back and forth between the different stories, weaving together a unity out of fragmentary episodes.

In *The Lower Depths*, using long takes and composition in depth, Kurosawa was able to present several events within one frame, a technique used by Jacques Tati and directors like William Wyler and Jean Renoir.

Rashomon, which attempts to chronicle one event from the viewpoint of four participants, was clearly an innovative departure in narrative structure when it appeared in 1950. Incorporating a series of flashbacks within a frame story (the men at the Rashomon gate), the film presents four contradictory tales which cannot be reconciled into one version of truth. The emphasis on relative knowledge (rendered both thematically and formally in this film) and the demands placed upon the viewer by Kurosawa's refusal to offer a correct reading, forms the basis for the film's reputation as a modern work of art in the pre-Godardian era.

Ikiru presents a more complicated narrative structure, interweaving past and present in an intricate pattern with references to the future provided by the narrator. By moving back and forth in time, Kurosawa provides ironic distance on the events which could not be accomplished by a chronological presentation. Like *High and Low*, the film divides into two parts: Watanabe's life and his funeral, although in this work the two halves are not equal.

In his book on Kurosawa (#269), Donald Richie has devised a scheme revealing how all Kurosawa films follow a pattern whose ultimate end is character revelation. He divides Kurosawa's films into two types: those which he calls "theme and variation" and those which he refers to as "sonata-form." He demonstrates, using eleven works, how Kurosawa introduces a theme, restates and develops it and closes with a coda. He also notes the cyclical structure of many Kurosawa films — "the return to the beginning with a difference." The reiteration of the opening image at the end of the film characterizes over half of Kurosawa's works.

Eastern/Western

Critics, both in Japan and elsewhere, often refer to Kurosawa's work as Western. There is some basis for such an evaluation. Most specifically it is Kurosawa's concentration on character and his belief in the value of individual action that reflects his occidental outlook. As opposed to most Japanese films which stress accommodation, Kurosawa heroes seek to change the world. And whereas Japanese culture stresses group participation and duty to one's family, work, and institutionalized society, Kurosawa protagonists act as individuals, their commitment to society arising from moral concern not obligation.

On the other hand, Kurosawa scholar Donald Richie defends Kurosawa's work as Japanese. Drawing on the tenets of Zen and the concept of Bushido, he notes the importance of self-determination, moral action, and continual spiritual growth. For Richie these elements, purely Japanese in origin, are part of the essence of Kurosawa's work.

Critics, in their haste to classify Kurosawa as Western, often seem misled by Kurosawa's film style, which shares much with traditional Hollywood filmmaking. In truth, this is the dominant film style in Japan as well as Hollywood and the assumption that Ozu and Mizoguchi are more Japanese is blatantly false. Both directors developed a highly personal style which is more idiosyncratic than Japanese.

Critics have looked for Japanese theatrical influences on Kurosawa's work. However, on only two occasions has he turned toward the traditional arts of Kabuki and Noh. In his early film, *The Men Who Tread on the Tiger's Tail*, he drew upon a text well-known in both schools of drama, and incorporated songs, dances and presentation.

However, it is with *The Throne of Blood*, that Kurosawa consciously set out to do a film based on the stylization of the Noh drama. To Donald Richie, he said "Essentially ... I am very Japanese. I like Japanese ceramics, Japanese painting — but I like the Noh best of all.... I've never much cared for the Kabuki, perhaps because I like Noh so much. I like it because it is the real heart, the core of all Japanese drama. Its degree of compression is extreme, and it is full of symbols, full of subtlety."[13] "I decided upon the techniques of the Noh, because in Noh, style and story are one. I wanted to use the way Noh actors have of moving their bodies, the way they have of walking, and the general composition which the Noh stage provides."[14] As for *Rashomon*, except for the female medium, there are no elements reflective of the traditional Japanese theater arts.

Kurosawa's direction tends to range from the highly naturalistic (*Ikiru*) to the very broad (*The Hidden Fortress*). Much Japanese cinema is highly melodramatic. This distinguishes the action films as well as the dramas. Thus, what has struck Western critics as excessive or sentimental in Kurosawa's films falls well within the boundaries of the norm in Japan.

Categorizing Kurosawa as Eastern or Western is as futile as trying to unravel the truth in *Rashomon*. Kurosawa's work is a synthesis of many influences. Clearly he has borrowed much from Western art and literature, but like most alien elements within the Japanese culture, these adoptions have been absorbed and transformed into something uniquely Japanese. Commenting on the debate, Kurosawa has remarked in 1960, "I haven't read one foreign review of anything I've done which hasn't read false meanings into it. But the Japanese critics go on and on about how Western I am. And mainly just because I do my own cutting and happen to prefer a fast tempo and am really interested in people. That's the thing about most Japanese films — they don't really give a damn about people. Then when they get done they call it 'artless simplicity' and terribly Japanese..."[15]

Perhaps the final word is best expressed by the opinion of Joan Mellen who states, "He [Kurosawa] is one of the few artists to achieve international communication while at the same time remaining true to his own highly distinctive and insular national culture."[16]

NOTES

1. Charles Higham, "Kurosawa's Humanism," *Kenyon Review*, vol. 27, no. 4, Autumn, 1965, p. 739.
2. Donald Richie, *The Films of Akira Kurosawa* (Berkeley: University of California Press, 1970), p. 115.
3. Marty Gliserman, "*Dodes' Ka-Den*," *Jump Cut*, no. 6, March-April, 1975, p. 1.
4. Joan Mellen, "*Dodeskaden*: A Renewal," *Cinema*, vol. 7, no. 2, issue no. 31, Spring, 1972, p. 22.
5. Donald Richie, "A Personal Record," *Film Quarterly*, vol. 14, no. 1, Fall, 1960, p. 20.
6. Joan Mellen, "The Epic Cinema of Kurosawa," *Take One*, vol. 3, no. 4, June, 1972, p. 19.

7. Barbara Wolf, "On Akira Kurosawa," *The Yale Review*, vol. 64, no. 2, 1974, p. 219.
8. Akira Iwasaki, "Kurosawa and His Work," *Japan Quarterly*, vol. 12, no. 1, January-March, 1965, p. 62.
9. Richie, *The Films of Akira Kurosawa*, p. 114.
10. *Ibid.*, p. 182.
11. Akira Kurosawa, "Why Mifune's Beard Won't Be Red," *Cinema*, vol. 2, no. 2, July, 1964, p. 40.
12. Richie, *The Films of Akira Kurosawa*, p. 185.
13. *Ibid.*, p. 117.
14. Donald Richie, "Kurosawa on Kurosawa," *Sight and Sound*, vol. 33, no. 4, Autumn, 1964, p. 201.
15. Richie, "A Personal Record," *Film Quarterly*, pp. 20 and 22.
16. Joan Mellen, *Voices From the Japanese Cinema* (New York: Liveright, 1975), p. 42.

The Films: Synopsis, Credits and Notes

1 SANSHIRO SUGATA [Sugata Sanshiro], 1943

    Producer: Keiji Matsuzaki (Toho)
    Director: Akira Kurosawa
    Screenplay: Akira Kurosawa, Based on the Novel *Sugata Sanshiro* by Tsuneo Tomita
    Photography: Akira Mimura
    Lighting: Masaki Onuma
    Art Direction: Masao Totsuka
    Scenario: Akira Kurosawa
    Music: Seichi Suzuki
    Sound: Tomohisa Higuchi
    Editors: Toshio Goto and Akira Kurosawa
    Cast: Susumu Fujita (Sanshiro Sugata), Denjiro Okochi (Shogoro Yano, his Father), Takashi Shimura (Hansuke Murai), Yukiko Todoroki (Sayo or Otomi, his Daughter), Yoshio Kosugi (Saburo Momma, the Jujitsu Teacher), Ranko Hanai (Osumi, his Daughter), Ryunosuke Tsukigata (Gennosuke Higaki), Akitake Kono (Yoshima or Yoshimaro Dan), Soshi Kiyokawa (Yujiro Toda), Kunio Mita (Kohei Tsuzaki), Akira Nakamura (Toranosuki Niiseki), Sugisaku Aoyama (Tsunetami Iimura), Kuninori Kodo (Priest), Ichiro Sugai (Police Chief), Michisaburo Segawa (Hatta), Eisaburo Sakauchi (Nemoto), Hajime Hikari (Torakichi)
    Distribution: Toho
    Running Time: 80 Minutes
    Released: March 25, 1943
    Other Titles: *Judo Saga, La légende de judo — I*

Synopsis

Edo. 1882. Young Sugata inquires where he can find the Shimnei jujitsu teacher. The jujitsu students heatedly discuss the new art of judo and their desire to defeat Shogoro Yano, the judo master. At night the students wait for Yano. One by one they attack, are thrown, and land in the nearby water. Sugata, impressed by Yano's superior skill, throws away his geta and pulls Yano home in a rickshaw.

Time passes marked by changing weather and the varying happenstance of Sugata's geta. Following a raucous fight in the gay quarter where Sugata takes on a sumo wrestler, he returns shamefacedly to his teacher's quiet house. The teacher admonishes him, saying that though he is strong, he does not know life. Life is truth and regret and only then can one know death. Impulsively Sugata opens a shoji screen and jumps into the lotus pond. Clinging to a pole, he stays there through the night. The teacher points out that his refusal to speak or to come out is stubbornness, not enlightenment.

In the morning Sugata sees a beautiful lotus flower and comes out of the mud, leaving the post to which he has clung as to life.

While washing laundry Sugata is approached by Gennosuke Higaki, a dandyfied Japanese who sports the latest Western fashions. Higaki wants to fight Sugata, but Yano refuses to allow a confrontation. [Sayo, the daughter of Higaki's jujitsu teacher comes to visit. Sayo is disturbed by his attention.]

A challenge arrives at the judo school and Sugata is chosen to combat Saburo Momma. People pack the hall to watch Sugata throw his opponent.

Sayo's father, Hansuke Murai, prepares to fight Sugata. In the street Sugata sees that Momma's house is up for sale. [Cut footage.] Momma's daughter Osumi tries to attack Sugata with a knife, but is disarmed. Near a temple Sugata observes a beautiful, young woman at prayer. Later he helps her fix her shoe. The two continue to see one another and eventually Sugata learns that the girl is Sayo, Murai's daughter.

When the match with Murai arrives, Sugata confesses to a priest his reluctance to fight Sayo's father. The priest tells him he must be pure as in the lotus pond. The match begins. Although initially Murai manages to throw Sugata several times, eventually Murai is so badly defeated that he must be carried out.

Sugata visits Murai while he is recovering. Higaki enters casting a pall over the atmosphere. Higaki delivers a challenge. The letter sets a fight for December 26, at 8:00 at Ueno. The fight is to be to the death. As Sugata reads the letter the sound of the wind fills the room.

Sugata now stands on a desolate, moon-lit plain, singing as he awaits Higaki. The sound of the wind grows louder and the clouds rush by above. The men fight in the tall grass and Higaki succeeds in locking Sugata in a neck grip. Sugata's eyes close. When they open he sees a cloud transform into a lotus blossom. Regaining his strength, he overcomes Higaki.

After the battle Sugata decides to go away to reflect. Sayo rides a short way with him on the train. Sugata promises to return soon.

Note

In March, 1944, 1,856 feet were cut from *Sanshiro Sugata* to conform to Japanese government regulations. This was done without Kurosawa's consent. Later efforts were made to find the missing footage, but due to wartime confusion, the material was never found. Toho Studios, however, released a reconstructed version in 1952, which supplies titles for the missing narrative and indicates where footage was deleted. These sections are bracketed in the synopsis.

During the American Occupation, *Sanshiro Sugata* was withdrawn from general circulation because the film expressed feudalistic ideas of loyalty.

2 THE MOST BEAUTIFUL [*Ichiban Utsukushiku*], 1944

Producer:	Motohiko Ito (Toho)
Director:	Akira Kurosawa
Screenplay:	Akira Kurosawa
Photography:	Joji Ohara
Art Direction:	Teruaki Abe
Scenario:	Akira Kurosawa
Music:	Seichi Suzuki
Cast:	Takashi Shimura (Factory Production Head), Ichiro Sugai (His Assistant), Yoko Yaguchi, Koyuri Tanima, Takako Irie, Toshiko Hattori (Girls)
Distribution:	Toho
Running Time:	85 Minutes
Released:	April 13, 1944
Other Titles:	*Most Beautifully, Le plus doux, Le plus beau.*

Synopsis

World War II. At an optical plant scores of young women live and work, doing their part for the war effort. The day consists of long, quiet hours of tedious work, grinding, polishing, and checking lenses and binoculars, followed by more relaxed moments in the dormitory-style dining room or sleeping rooms. Time is also set aside for military drills with flute and drum and volley ball games; the former inspire the women to work harder and the latter boost their morale. The girls are cared for by a kindly, older woman who serves as a surrogate mother.

Unexpectedly one girl falls sick and must return home. When her father comes to fetch her all of the young women break down into tears. However, life at the factory continues and the productivity chart begins to climb. Another girl accidentally falls from a roof top and must be confined to the hospital until her leg mends. As the days wear on the girls lose interest in their work and production declines. However, sparked by the enthusiasm of one serious-minded young lady — a natural leader — and the chance to release their energy on the ball court, the women finally perk up again.

Homesickness continues to plague the group and many become listless and disinterested. One even allows a machine to run haywire. The male supervisors try without success to inspire patriotism. When the older woman travels home for a visit, the girls miss her and easily express their tears.

Upon returning, the woman hears about the young girl leader who negligently allowed a lens to go through production without the proper check. There ensues a long sequence which follows the young lady as she works through the night, sorting through thousands of lenses until she locates the missing one. Next day, exhausted with fatigue, she emerges from the workroom, pleased by a job well done. Outside her supervisors and co-workers await her.

Life returns to normal. Production remains high. When the young leader hears about her mother's death, she declines the opportunity to return home. Joining the rest of the women, she returns to her job. On the soundtrack the voices of women singing is heard.

3   SANSHIRO SUGATA PART TWO [*Zoku Sugata Sanshiro*], 1945

Producer:	Motohiko Ito (Toho)
Director:	Akira Kurosawa
Screenplay:	Akira Kurosasa, Based on the Novel *Sugata Sanshiro* by Tsuneo Tomita
Photography:	Hiroshi Suzuki
Art Direction:	Kazuo Kubo
Scenario:	Akira Kurosawa
Music:	Seichi Suzuki
Cast:	Susumu Fujita (Sanshiro Sugata), Denjiro Okochi (Shogoro), Aritake Kono (Yoshima Dan), Ryunosuke Tsukigata (Gennosuke), Yukiko Todoroki (Sayo), Soshi Kiyokawa (Yujiro Toda)
Distribution:	Toho
Running Time:	83 Minutes
Released:	May 3, 1945
Other Titles:	*Judo Saga — II, La légende de judo — II*.

Synopsis

Edo. 1887. Riding into town in a local rickshaw, an American sailor persists in abusing the young driver. Finally, Sugata, who has witnessed the event, throws the sailor into the nearby water. The young boy, grateful and impressed by Sugata's strength determines to study judo like his new idol.

A Japanese government representative, absurd looking in his foreign clothes, comes to take Sugata to a boxing match. In English the Japanese man introduces both fighters to an aging jujitsu man and a Western boxer. The audience, mostly foreign, is noisy and raucous. Sugata interrupts the event to speak to the jujitsu fighter. Offended by his choice of jujitsu over judo, he learns that he fights to stay alive. Satisfied with this answer, Sugata leaves.

Sugata visits a priest and spends the night meditating. As evening dissolves into morning he is embarrassed to discover he had inadvertently fallen asleep during the night. Turning to the priest to apologize, Sugata is amused and relieved to discover the priest is soundly asleep as well.

Later Sugata agrees to fight a foreign boxer himself. The fight is preceded by a long procession to the hall accompanied by a band. The audience is divided into Japanese men wearing black and American sailors. Self-consciously Sugata rubs his head. The crowd is hostile to Sugata and calls out for blood, but Sugata easily defeats his opponent, first pulling him around in a circle and then throwing him to the floor. Reluctant to take the award money, he finally accepts it and then gives it away.

At home three men come to visit. One bemusedly knocks him. Sayo, the young girl who loves Sugata, weeps. Together the two walk through the cemetery with the priest and sit in front of the chrysanthemums.

Later two men, both menacing, come to call. They are the brothers of the judo expert who Sugata defeated five years before. A challenge is delivered and Sugata waits for the men on a snowy plain outside the city.

The brothers arrive. One has long, flowing hair and looks quite mad. The two men, like characters in a Noh play, gesture and grunt, as if in a drama. Swinging at Sugata, one brother, a karate champion, misses him and fells a tree. The howls of the fighters echo against the mountains. Finally Sugata throws and injures his karate opponent.

The three then build a fire and bed down in the snow for the evening. Covering the injured man with a blanket, Sugata then falls asleep. During the night the crazed brother steals over to Sugata planning to kill him with his knife. But Sugata, hearing a girl's voice in his dream, smiles. This disorients the villain so that he withdraws frightened and crying. Completely oblivious of his narrow escape, Sugata arises and smiles happily.

Note

Like *Sanshiro Sugata*, *Sanshiro Sugata — Part Two* was also banned during the Occupation.

4 THE MEN WHO TREAD ON THE TIGER'S TAIL [*Tora No O O Fumu Otokotachi*], 1945

Producer:	Motohiko Ito (Toho)
Director:	Akira Kurosawa
Screenplay:	Akira Kurosawa, Based on the Kabuki drama *Kanjincho*
Photography:	Takeo Ito
Art Direction:	Kazuo Kubo
Scenario:	Akiro Kurosawa
Music:	Tadashi Hattori
Sound:	Keiji Hasebe
Cast:	Hanshiro Iwai (Yoshitsune or Yoshisune, The Lord), Susumu Fujita (Togashi, the Magistrate), Kenichi Enomoto (the Porter), Denjiro Okochi (Benkei, Chief Vassal), Masayuki Mori, Takashi Shimura, Aritake Kono, Yoshio Kosugi, Dekao Yoko Kamei, Kataoka, Ise, Suruga, Hidachibo, Vassals), Seji Kiyokawa (Togashi's Aide)
Distribution:	Toho
Running Time:	60 Minutes
Released:	April 24, 1952
U. S. Release:	January, 1960
Other Titles:	*They Who Step on the Tiger's Tail*, *Walkers on the Tiger's Tail*, *They Who Step on the Tail of the Tiger*, *Sur la queue du tigre*, *Les hommes qui marchèrent sur la queue du tigre*

Synopsis

During the 12th century civil struggles in Japan, Yoshitsune, a general of the Genji clan, is forced to flee from his brother Yoritomo. In a forest he travels with his five loyal retainers and Benkei, his personal bodyguard. All are disguised as monks. Along the way they are joined by a comic, chattering porter who slowly discovers their real identity.

Before approaching the border guard in Kaga Province, Yoshitsune changes into the clothes of a common porter, hiding his face beneath a large straw hat. This scene is accompanied by a song which describes the transformation. The group appears at the barrier camp requesting alms for a temple in Nara. They are greeted by Togashi, the provincial magistrate. Togashi's aide is suspicious of the group and wants to arrest them. Benkei requests permission to offer a last prayer. Togashi, disarmed by Benkei's religious resolution, grants permission. Reading from a blank scroll, Benkei delivers a long Buddhist invocation. During the chanting Togashi dozes. Afterwards Togashi questions Benkei further, especially regarding why the monks carry swords. Throughout this trial, the tension and fear is registered on the porter's face. Satisfied with Benkei's responses, Togashi decides to let the group pass and even agrees to make a contribution to the sect.

The group prepares to leave while listening to a song from the Kabuki Theater which cautions them not to move too quickly, but slowly as if 'treading on a tiger's tail.' At the last moment Togashi's aide thinks he recognizes Yoshitsune. Immediately Benkei pushes Yoshitsune to the ground and beats him with a stick. Benkei also accuses the aide of thieving. Everyone draws swords, ready for action.

Togashi must decide the case. Aware of the true facts, he is so touched by Benkei's loyalty that he allows the group to continue, stating that as no vassal would ever strike a lord, the group must be innocent.

Arriving at a clearing, all laugh with relief, except Benkei who kneels and weeps. He cannot forgive himself for striking his lord, but Yoshitsune absolves him. A messenger arrives from Togashi with saké as a form of apology. The danger averted, everyone drinks in friendship and humanity. Many cups later, everyone is drunk. Benkei sings a farewell song while the porter dances. Later the porter awakens in a meadow alone and finely dressed. He dances off into the distance.

Note

In 1944 Kurosawa was asked by the Japanese government to film the well known Noh and Kabuki story, *The Men Who Tread on the Tiger's Tail*. Since all Kabuki Theaters were closed, the militarists hoped to provide audiences with traditional entertainment which emphasized feudal values, especially loyalty to one's superiors. However, because of changes which Kurosawa made in the treatment, most specifically the addition of the porter, a low comic character, the government refused to release the film. They felt that Kurosawa's version ridiculed and debased the very ideals they had hoped to propagate.

After the war the American military forces again banned the film on the basis that such a feudalistic narrative was in opposition to the democratic ideas of the Occupation. The film was finally released in Japan in 1952.

*5   THOSE WHO MAKE TOMORROW [*Asu O Tsukuru Hitobito*], 1946

Producers: Ryo Takei, Sojiro Motoki, Keiji Matsuzaki, and Tomoyuki Tanaka (Toho)

Directors:	Kajiro Yamamoto, Hideo Sekigawa, and Akira Kurosawa
Photography:	Takeo Ito, Mitsui Miura, and Taiichi Kankura
Scenario:	Yusaku Yamagata and Kajiro Yamamoto
Cast:	Kenji Susukida (Father), Chieko Takehisa (Mother), Chieko Nakakita (Elder Sister), Mitsue Tachibana (Younger Sister), Masayuki Mori (Chauffeur), Sumie Tsubaki (His Wife), Ichiro Chiba (Lightman), Hyo Kitazawa (Director), Itoko Kono (Actress), Takashi Shimura (Theater Manager), Masao Shimizu (Section Chief), Yuriko Hamada and Sayuri Tanima (Dancing Girls)
Distribution:	Toho
Running Time:	81 Minutes
Released:	May 2, 1946
Other Titles:	*Ceux qui font l'avenir, Ceux qui bâtissent l'avenir*

Synopsis

1946. The Okomoto family stands at the center of the action. The father is a minor department-head in the metal industry. Both of his daughters work in a movie studio: Yoshiko as a scriptgirl, Aiko as a dancer. The railroad employee Hori and his wife also live in the Okomoto family house. Hori's child, who lives in the country with relatives, is suffering from pneumonia. The railroad workers have gone on strike, and since Hori is busy with union work, he can't go to visit his ailing son. In the Okomoto family, only Yoshiko is on the side of the union. At first her father doesn't want to know anything about it. He still has his job....

There are discussions everywhere about the problem of union organization. Unemployment and inflation are prevalent. The debates also gain ground in the world of the studio workers. When the actors there learn of the railroad workers' strike, they declare their solidarity with them.

The dancers act otherwise. Although they work under horrible conditions, their argument against joining the union is, "We are artists, not workers." The conflicts meanwhile come to a crisis, and when a sick dancer is fired, the dancers also join the workers' movement. Okomoto is threatened with dismissal. He can't understand it at first. Nevertheless, when the threat is carried out, he also joins the great procession of striking and demonstrating workers. This procession grows constantly.

There are a great many gatherings and announcements of solidarity. In one of these, Yoshiko comes to the speaker's stand. She tells the assembled workers about the death of Hori's son, and his inability to see the boy because of his exclusive devotion to the workers' movement. His attitude meets with great approbation, not least from Okomoto himself. On May 1st, he sets out with his family for the coming May Day marches.

Adapted and translated by Robert Kenyon from a text by Reinhard Priessnitz by permission of Oesterreichisches Filmmuseum; Vienna, Austria.

6 NO REGRETS FOR OUR YOUTH [*Waga Seishun Ni Kuinashi*], 1946

Producer:	Keiji Matsuzaki (Toho)
Director:	Akira Kurosawa

Photography:	Asakazu Nakai
Lighting:	Chochiro Ishii
Art Direction:	Keiji Kitagawa
Scenario:	Eijiro Hisaita and Akira Kurosawa
Music:	Tadashi Hattori
Sound:	Isamu Suzuki
Cast:	Denjiro Okochi (Professor Yagihara), Eiko Miyoshi (His Wife), Setsuko Hara (Yukie, his Daughter), Susumu Fujita (Ryukicki Noge), Kuninori Kodo (His Father), Haruko Sugimura (His Mother), Aritake Kono (Itokawa), Takashi Shimura (Dokuichigo, Police Commissioner), Masao Shimizu (Hakozaki), Haruo Tanaka Ichiro Chiba, Isamu Yonekura, Noboru Takagi, Hiroshi Sano (Students)
Distribution:	Toho
Running Time:	110 Minutes
Released:	October 29, 1946
Other Titles:	No Regrets for My Youth, Je ne regrette rien de ma jeunesse, Je ne regrette pas ma jeunesse

Synopsis

Kyoto. 1933. On a hill outside the city Yukie Yagihara sits with her university friends Noge and Itokawa, singing freedom songs and frolicking in the outdoors. Despite the happy mood, Noge warns that Fascism is like a coming storm and refers to the Manchurian Incident.

At home the three discuss government oppression of university professors like Yukie's father. All who support freedom of speech are being labeled as Communists. A montage sequence documents the student protests in universities across the country. At The Imperial University of Kyoto, Professor Yagihara delivers a speech of hope and defeat before an assembled body of students.

At home Itokawa's mother begs her son to give up his fight and finish his degree. She argues that without a father and any income, he must graduate and find a good job. Finally Itokawa decides to stay at the university. The decision disturbs Yukie, who feels that he has betrayed the cause. Meanwhile, news reaches the Yagihara household that Noge has disappeared.

1938. Times have changed. Most students now wear military uniforms. Professor Yagihara, dismissed from the university, now gives free legal advice to the poor. Yukie decides she will marry Itokawa, however, she changes her mind when Noge appears.

Disillusioned by the knowledge of Noge's imprisonment, Itokawa's efforts to win him a probation, and his present job as a military assistant, she decides to move to Tokyo. Although her mother opposes the move, her father tells her she must find her own way and fight for freedom.

1941. Accidentally Yukie meets Itokawa on the street. She learns that Noge, now a journalist, is also in Tokyo. Seasons pass. One day Noge chances to see Yukie in front of his office. The old feelings are rekindled. The two marry.

Shortly thereafter, Noge and Yukie are arrested as spies. She is imprisoned, but refuses to give any information. A radio broadcast announces the Japanese attack on Pearl Harbor. Professor Yagihara comes to take Yukie home and decides to stand for Noge, despite Itokawa's warning against such action. The professor replies that Noge is teaching him what he should do.

Yukie learns that Noge has died suddenly in prison. She decides to visit his parents in a remote Japanese village. Their home is shuttered against the world and a sign reads, "The house of a spy." She begs to be permitted to stay and work. At first suspicious, they finally concede. Slowly Yukie learns the harsh realities of farm life and instills pride and courage in Noge's parents, who have been defeated by shame and humiliation.

After the war Professor Yagihara addresses the students at Kyoto University once again. He proclaims, "the day belongs to Noge." At home Yukie visits with her parents, but announces her plans to return to the village and to live a life she can be proud of.

Note

No Regrets For Our Youth is based upon an authentic incident. In 1933, Professor Yukitoki Takikawa was forced to resign his position at Kyoto University for Communistic leanings. This had repercussions throughout the country. Later in 1944, his former pupil Hidemi Ozaki was executed for espionage activities. The characters of Professor Yagihara and Noge are based on Takikawa and Ozaki.

*7 ONE WONDERFUL SUNDAY [*Subarashiki Nichiyobi*], 1947

Producer:	Sojiro Motogi (Toho)
Director:	Akira Kurosawa
Photography:	Asakuzu Nakai
Lighting:	Kuichiro Kishida
Art Direction:	Kazuo Kubo
Scenario:	Keinosuke Uegusa and Akira Kurosawa
Music:	Tadashi Hattori
Sound:	Juen Yasue
Cast:	Isao Numasaki (Yuzo), Chieko Nakakita (Masako), Ichiro Sugai (Yamiya, the black-marketeer), Midori Ariyama (Sono, his mistress), Masao Shimizu (Bar Owner), Sachio Sakai (Ticket Man), Toshi Mori (Master of Apartment), Tokuji Kobayashi (Fat Man), Shiro Mizutani (Waif), Zeko Nakamura (Shop Owner), Atsushi Watanabe (Man), Aguri Hidaka (Dancer), Katao Numazaki (Bakery Owner), Ichiro Namiki (Pavement Photographer), Toppa Utsumi (Pavement Photographer)
Distribution:	Toho
Running Time:	108 Minutes
Released:	June 25, 1947
Other Titles:	*Wonderful Sunday, Un merveilleux dimanche*

Synopsis

Tokyo. 1947. Sunday. At a crowded train station Masako meets her boyfriend Yuzo. She bubbles with joy. He is depressed and angry because he has no money and cannot marry until they find a place to live. He remembers fondly the happy days before the war.

Together the lovers look at a model house. They overhear a mention of a room for rent. Tracking down the address, they find an ugly 9' × 12' room which is still beyond their small means.

Forgetting all problems for awhile, the two play baseball with a group of children. Then they look up an old war buddy who now runs a dance hall, but are unable to make contact. Next they sit in the park eating rice balls. Yuzo contemplates becoming a black marketeer.

Masako and Yuzo visit the zoo where animals are happy and know nothing of inflation. Deciding to attend a concert, the two get to the box-office only to discover that all the tickets have been purchased by a man who plans to resell them at a profit. In anger Yuzo attacks the man and is subsequently beaten up by the man's buddies.

The two return to Yuzo's apartment. Yuzo wants to make love, but Masako hesitates. When she finally begins to unbutton her coat, Yuzo realizes the selfishness of his motives and lets her go.

Together the two go downtown to a bakery. When the bill is higher than expected, Yuzo is forced to leave his coat. The two dream of a bakery of their own, The Hyacinth, the people's restaurant.

At night Masako and Yuzo visit an empty park. Under the moon they play on swings like happy children. Climbing over a fence they land in an open-air concert band shell. Masako sits on a bench while Yuzo pretends to conduct an orchestra. Both listen for the music but hear only the whistling of the wind. Masako faces the audience and pleads for warmth and applause. Suddenly the strains of Schubert are heard on the soundtrack. Masako cries.

8 DRUNKEN ANGEL [*Yoidore Tenshi*], 1948

Producer:	Sojiro Motoki (Toho)
Director:	Akira Kurosawa
Photography:	Takeo Ito
Lighting:	Kinzo Yoshizawa
Art Direction:	So Matsuyama
Scenario:	Keinosuke Uegusa and Akira Kurosawa
Music:	Fumio Hayasaka
Sound:	Wataru Konuma
Cast:	Takashi Shimura (Sanada, the Doctor), Toshiro Mifune (Matsunaga, the Gangster), Reisaburo Yamamoto (Okada, the Gang-boss), Chieko Nakakita (Miyo, the Nurse), Michiyo Kogure (Nanae, Matsunaga's Mistress), Noriko Sengoku (Gin, the Bar-girl), Eitaro Shindo (Takahama, the Doctor's Friend), Choko Iida (Old Servant), Taiji Tonoyama (Shop Owner), Katao Kawasaki (Master of the Flower Shop), Sachio Sakai (Young Hoodlum), Yoshiko Kuga (Girl), Shizuko Kasagi (Singer), Masao Shimizu (Boss), Sumire Shiroki (Anego)
Distribution:	Toho
Running Time:	102 Minutes
Released:	April 27, 1948
U.S. Release:	December, 1959
Other Titles:	*A Drunken Angel, L'Ange ivre.*

Synopsis

Tokyo. 1948. Living in a poor district aside a fetid swamp, the aging, disheveled Dr. Sanada administers to the neighborhood. Enraged by the poverty, disease and corruption he sees in postwar Japan, he takes his anger out on his patients and loses himself in drink. Sanada's prize patient is a young schoolgirl who is fighting a battle against tuberculosis.

One day Matsunaga, a local racketeer who pushes his weight around the neighborhood comes to Sanada to have a bullet removed. Sanada discovers he has an advanced case of tuberculosis and warns him against alcohol. Angry, Matsunaga runs off to the local dance hall. Sanada follows. The two drink together and Sanada urges him to see an old classmate, now a successful physician, for an x-ray. At the clinic, after a struggle with his own fears, Matsunaga finally brings Sanada the x-ray. Drunk, but ready to be cured, Matsunaga begins to think about a new life. Simultaneously Okada, the ex-neighborhood boss, returns from prison.

Okada usurps Matsunaga's position as well as his mistress, Nanae, who leaves Matsunaga after he has a lung hemorrhage. Matsunaga goes to live with Sanada, who tells him his lungs are like the swamp. At night he dreams he is chasing his own corpse.

Unwilling to be supplanted, Matsunaga breaks into the apartment where Okada is living with Nanae. The two men struggle amidst ladders and buckets of white paint until eventually Okada delivers a fatal stab. Matsunaga staggers out to the roof, falls onto a laundry platform, and dies. Later, Gin, a bar-girl who has loved Matsunaga, sits with a small white box which contains his ashes. She and Sanada discuss the dead gangster. Sanada is still angry with the world, but encouraged by the young girl who has courageously won her fight against tuberculosis.

9   THE QUIET DUEL [*Shizukanaru Ketto*], 1949

        Producers: Sojiro Motogi and Hisao Ichikawa (Daiei)
        Director: Akira Kurosawa
        Screenplay: Senkichi Taniguchi and Akira Kurosawa, Based on a Play by Kazuo Kikuta
        Photography: Shoichi Aisaka
        Lighting: Tsunekichi Shibata
        Art Direction: Koichi Imai
        Scenario: Senkichi Taniguchi and Akira Kurosawa
        Music: Akira Ifukube
        Sound: Mitsuo Hasegawa
        Stills: Isamu Shiina
        Editor: Masanori Tsuji
        Cast: Toshiro Mifune (Kyoji Fujisaki), Takashi Shimura (Konosuie Fujisaki, his Father), Miki Sanjo (Misao Matsumoto, Kyoji's Girlfriend), Kenjiro Uemura (Tatsuo or Susumu Nakada), Chieko Nakakita (Takiko Nakada, his Wife), Noriko Sengoku (Rui Minegishi, the Nurse), Jyunnosuke Miyazaki (Horiguchi), Isamu Yamaguchi (Nosaka), Shi-

geru Matsumoto (Appendicitis Boy), Hiroko Machida (Imai), Kan Takami (Laborer), Kisao Tobita (Typhoid Boy), Shigeyuki Miyajima (Officer), Tadashi Date (Appendicitis Boy's Father), Etsuko Sudo (Appendicitis Boy's Mother), Seiji Izumi (Policeman), Masateru Sasaki (Old Soldier), Kenichi Miyajima (Dealer), Yosuke Kudo (Boy), Yakuko Ikegami (Gaudy Female), Wakayo Matsumura (Pupil Nurse), Hatsuko Wakahara (Mii-chan)

Distribution: Daiei
Running Time: 95 Minutes
Released: March 13, 1949
Other Titles: *A Silent Duel, Le duel silencieux*

Synopsis

Pacific Front. 1944. During surgery, Kyoji Fujisaki, a young army doctor accidentally cuts his hand on a scalpel, but finishes the operation. Later Fujisaki discovers that the patient has an advanced case of syphilis. He warns the patient, Tatsuo Nakata, against spreading the disease.

After the war Fujisaki returns to Japan and takes up practice in his father's charity hospital. Because he has contracted Nakata's syphilis he decides not to marry his fiancee, Misao, who has waited for his return. Although he loves her, he also decides not to reveal his real reason for fear that she will decide to wait longer.

Working in the clinic is a pregnant apprentice nurse, Rui Minegishi, a former dance hall girl. Angry at all men, she distrusts Fujisaki's seeming humanitarianism and seeks to discredit him. She changes heart when she overhears him reveal his problems to his father. Rui subsequently decides to take the nurse's examination.

Seasons pass. Rui delivers her baby. Fujisaki is called to attend a police victim. He discovers that the attacker is none other than Nakata, his former patient, who has now married, infected his pregnant wife, and become a hopeless drunk. Fujisaki insists upon treating Nakata's wife. Misao comes to tell Fujisaki that she is about to marry someone else. Sadly, the two part. Takiko, Nakata's wife, has a premature delivery. Nakata arrives at the hospital drunk and angry. Fujisaki insists he enter the operating room. At the sight of his dead child, he breaks down totally and is committed to a sanitarium. Rui, secretly in love with Fujisaki and inspired by his self-sacrifice and dedication, decides to devote herself to medicine. Fujisaki, ennobled by suffering, pledges to help those even less fortunate than himself.

10   STRAY DOG [*Nora Inu*], 1949

Producer: Sojiro Motogi (Shintoho)
Director: Akira Kurosawa
Photography: Asakazu Nakai
Lighting: Choshiro Ishii
Art Direction: So Matsuyama
Scenario: Ryuzo Kikushima and Akira Kurosawa

Music:	Fumio Hayasaka
Sound:	Fumio Yanoguchi
Cast:	Toshiro Mifune (Murakami, the Detective), Takashi Shimura (Sato, the Head-detective), Ko Kimura (Yuro, the Criminal), Keiko Awaji (Harumi Namiki, his Girl), Reisaburo Yamamoto (Hondo, the Suspect), Noriko Sengoku (Girl), Gen Shimizu (Nakajima), Yasushi Nagata (Abe), Reikichi Kawamura (Ichikawa), Eiko Miyoshi (Harumi's Mother), Kazuko Motohashi (Mrs. Sato-Tomi), Teruko Kishi (Ogin), Isao Kimura (Shinjiro Yusa), Eijiro Tono (Old Man of Wooden Tub Shop), Ayako Honma (Woman of Wooden Tub Shop), Yunosuke Ito (Manager of The Bluebird Theater), Choko Iida (Lady Manager of the Kogetsu Hotel), Minoru Chiaki (Young Man of the Bluebird Theater), Masao Shimizu (Nakamura), Hajime Izu (Lab Assistant), Kan Yanagiya (Cop), Ichiro Sugai (Manager of the Yayoi Hotel), Eizo Tanaka (Old Doctor), Shiro Mizutani (Punk), Isao Ubukata (Sei-san), Fujio Nagahama (Manager of the Sakura Hotel), Akira Ubukata (Police Doctor), Kokuten Kodo (Old Man of the Apartment Building), Rikie Sanjyo (Manager's Wife), Aso Mie (Woman of the Pin-ball Parlor), Haruko Toyama (Kintaro-Geisha), Haruko Toda (Madam of the Azuma Hotel)
Distribution:	Shintoho (acquired by Toho in 1959)
Running Time:	122 Minutes
Released:	October 17, 1949
U.S. Release:	March, 1964
Other Title:	*Le chien enragé*

Synopsis

Summer. 1949. After target practice, police Detective Murakami boards a crowded bus. As he disembarks, he realizes his pistol has been stolen. He chases a young man down a deserted street but loses him in the slum area. Next day he appears before his superior, Nakajimi, ready for punishment, but is told to look for his gun instead. While searching through criminal identification cards, he recognizes the woman who was standing next to him on the bus. He and Officer Ichikawa track her down, but she refuses to talk.

Undaunted, Murakami follows her through the afternoon until she breaks down and gives him a lead. She tells him to make contact with the secondhand gun dealers near the amusement park.

Wearing shabby clothes, Murakami stalks the likely areas of Tokyo night and day. Finally, wet and weary, he falls asleep in the street. A young ruffian asks him if he wants to buy a gun. He sends Murakami to the Conga Tea Shop where he immediately arrests a female suspect.

At the police station, the woman complains, but reveals little. Murakami is reprimanded for arresting her so quickly. Murakami learns that on the previous evening, a girl was shot during a robbery with a Colt revolver. Fearing it was his, Murakami goes to the shooting range to retrieve his bullet. Laboratory tests confirm his fears. Guilt-ridden, he wants to resign, but is assigned instead to the homicide case under senior Officer Sato, a kindly and totally professional man.

Sato questions the woman Murakami arrested and finally gets the name of the man to whom she lent the Colt. The two track him down to Korakuen Baseball Park. Vendors are alerted to watch for the suspected criminal. Finally he is recognized. At the front gate Sato arrests him, but unfortunately he no longer has the gun. They do discover, however, a rice ration book with the name of Shinjiro Yusa.

Murakami is consumed with the fear that something worse is about to happen. Meanwhile, Sato concerns himself with preventing another crime. The two men visit Yusa's home and search his room. They next visit the hotel where Yusa works and gain information from a friend. This leads to The Bluebird Theater and a line dancer named Harumi Namiki.

Finally, weary, Sato goes home to his family. The two men talk about the apres-guerre generation. Murakami expresses his sympathy for the poor like Yusa. Sato tells him he must keep his mind on society's victims and leave the criminal mind to the novelists.

A new case arrives. A woman has been killed by an armed robber; again it is Murakami's gun. Sato claims that killers are like mad dogs and must be hunted down. The two visit Harumi at her home. After much persuasion she agrees to help them. Sato tracks Yusa to the Yayoi Hotel. Overhearing a conversation, Yusa is forewarned and shoots Sato in a telephone booth.

Acting on information that Harumi provides, Murakami seeks out Yusa at a train station. A chase ensues. Yusa wounds Murakami, then the two struggle until both are exhausted. Finally Murakami handcuffs Yusa, who breaks down into tears. At the hospital Murakami sits with Sato who is recovering. The older man says it's always hard to forget your first case and tells Murakami that the best thing is just to go back to work.

11 SCANDAL [*Shubun*], 1950

Producer:	Takashi Koide (Shochiku)
Director:	Akira Kurosawa
Photography:	Toshio Ubukata
Art Direction:	Tatsuo Hamada
Scenario:	Ryuzo Kikushima and Akira Kurosawa
Music:	Fumio Hayasaka
Cast:	Toshiro Mifune (Ichiro Aoye), Yoshiko Yamaguchi (Miyako Saigo), Takashi Shimura (Hiruta, the Lawyer), Yoko Katsuragi (Masako, his Daughter), Noriko Sengoku (Sumie, Aoye's Model), Eitaro Ozawa (Hori, the Publisher), Bokuzen Hidari (Drunk), Kuninori Kodo (Farmer)
Distribution:	Shochiku
Running Time:	105 Minutes
Released:	April 30, 1950
Other Title:	*Scandale*

Synopsis

1950. While out painting in the mountain, Ichiro Aoye, a young Bohemian artist, meets a popular song star, Miyako Saigo. He gives her a ride on his motorcycle to a nearby inn. At the inn a group of photographers are provoked by Miyako's refusal to grant them an interview. They assuage their anger by snapping a picture of Miyako on a balcony with Aoye, which they plan to use as an expose in a scandal magazine, *Amour*.

A montage sequence showing posters and newspaper headlines covers the dissemination of the story. As the photographers celebrate their triumph, Aoye enters and slugs the publisher. He decides to bring the case to court, although Miyako refuses to join the suit. One evening, while painting, Aoye is visited by a meek, aging lawyer, Hiruta, who wants to take the case. Hiruta claims that he is outraged by the incursions against the individual in contemporary society. Aoye decides to consider the offer.

When Aoye returns Hiruta's visit, he discovers that the old man's office is a roof-top shack and that his young daughter Masako is dying of tuberculosis. Aoye appoints Hiruta as counsel.

When Hiruta visits Amour Publishers, he is easily scared off by their threats. He returns home defeated and drunk. Masako fears that her father will succumb to pressure. Aoye also has his doubts.

Ultimately Hiruta accepts a bribe from Amour Publishers to throw the case. Momentarily Hiruta wants to drop the case, but when Miyako joins the suit, he is unable to do so.

Aoye and Miyako visit Masako often, frequently bringing gifts. On Christmas Eve, Aoye arrives with a decorated tree. Hiruta remains outdoors, too guilt-ridden to enter the house. Drowning his sorrows at the local bar, he calls himself a "miserable dog" and "a scoundrel," but pledges that next year he'll be "a new man."

The case comes to trial. Hiruta is notably unprepared and consistently makes a fool of himself. Aoye brings flowers to Masako, but she is too ashamed of her father's behavior to accept such kindness. Aoye explains that Hiruta is weak, not evil, and assures her that in the end they will win.

At home Aoye runs his motorcycle to relieve his frustration at the results of the trial. Hiruta comes to announce that Masako is dead. Next day, closing arguments are given. Aoye speaks in his own defense, expressing his fears for putting too much faith in 'the law.' His opponents deliver an impressive speech. At last Hiruta rises; shaking and perspired, he takes the witness stand. He discloses a receipt for the ¥ 100,000 bribe. The court dissolves in turmoil. The defense concedes. Aoye is stunned. Realizing what such a disclosure will mean to Hiruta, he claims the birth of a new star.

12 RASHOMON, 1950

Producer:	Jingo Minoru (Later Titles: Produced by Masaichi Nagata) (Daiei Production)
Director:	Akira Kurosawa

Screenplay:	Shinobu Hashimoto and Akira Kurosawa, Based on Two Stories by Ryunosuke Akutagawa: "Rashomon" and "In a Grove"
Photography:	Kazuo Miyagawa
Lighting:	Kenichi Okamoto
Art Direction:	So Matsuyama
Scenario:	Shinobu Hashimoto and Akira Kurosawa
Music:	Fumio Hayasaka
Cast:	Toshiro Mifune (Tajomaru, the Bandit), Masayuki Mori (Takehiro, the Samurai), Machiko Kyo (Masago, his Wife), Takashi Shimura (Woodcutter), Minoru Chiaki (Priest), Kichijiro Ueda (Commoner), Daisuke Kato (Police-Agent), Fumiko Homma (Medium)
Distribution:	Daiei
Running Time:	88 Minutes
Released:	August 25, 1950
U.S. Release:	December 26, 1951

Synopsis

Kyoto. 12th century. During a rainstorm a priest, a woodcutter, and a commoner seek shelter inside the half-ruined Rashomon gate and discuss the strange murder case of a samurai warrior. The woodcutter tells how he discovered the corpse and several articles of clothing while working in the woods. The priest, who saw the man leading his wife who is seated upon a horse, recounts the testimony of Tajomaru, a bandit executed for the crime. A flashback reveals Tajomaru, tied in ropes, facing the court magistrate. (All witnesses look directly at the camera.) In a second flashback Tajomaru tells how he sees the couple pass and how the wife's beauty arouses his lust. Leaping after them, he lures the samurai deep into the woods with stories of hidden treasure. He binds the husband in ropes, forces the wife to observe his humiliation, and rapes her.

At first she fights like a cat, but finally gives herself to the bandit. After the rape, the woman insists that now one of the men must die. The two fight bravely until Tajomaru spears the husband. Tajomaru claims that when the fight was over, the woman had fled.

The woodcutter rejects Tajomaru's story as false. The priest then tells the wife's version. She claims that after the rape, her husband's eyes revealed his hatred toward her. With her dagger she cut his bonds, moving toward him until she fainted. When she awoke, the dagger was protruding from his chest. Grief stricken, she tried to drown herself in a nearby lake, but failed.

At the gate, the commoner remains cynical. The priest continues, this time recounting the dead man's version as told through a female medium. After the rape Tajomaru tried to comfort the sobbing wife, all the while urging her to run away with him. The wife agreed to go, but demanded that Tajomaru kill her husband first. Tajomaru is outraged. The wife fled and Tajomaru cut the captive's ropes. Shaken with sorrow, the husband took a dagger and stabbed himself. Hours later he felt someone remove the dagger.

At the gate the woodcutter again declares that all three accounts are lies. He claims to have witnessed the whole event, remaining silent to stay uninvolved.

The woodcutter then tells his tale. After the rape Tajomaru begged the woman to forgive him, even promising her marriage. She demanded that the two fight, vowing to take the winner. Reluctantly the husband agreed, and the two men engaged in a cautious, cowardly fight which Tajomaru eventually won. The husband begged for his life, but Tajomaru was unmoved. As in previous versions, the wife ran off.

After all four tales, the commoner is more convinced than ever of man's base nature. He even accuses the woodcutter of stealing the missing dagger. As the storm subsides the three men find an abandoned infant, which the woodcutter decides to adopt. The priest, his faith in humanity restored, leaves the gate as the sun appears in the sky.

13   THE IDIOT [*Hakuchi*], 1951

Producer:	Takashi Koide (Shochiku)
Director:	Akira Kurosawa
Screenplay:	Eijiro Hisaita and Akira Kurosawa, Based on Feodor Dostoyevsky's novel *The Idiot*
Photography:	Toshio Ubukata
Lighting:	Akio Tamura
Art Direction:	So Matsuyama
Scenario:	Eijiro Hisaita and Akira Kurosawa
Music:	Fumio Hayasaka
Sound:	Yoshisaburo Imo
Settings:	Shohei Sekine
Decoration:	Ushitaro Shimada
Editor:	Yoshi Sugihara
Cast:	Masayuki Mori (Kameda), Toshiro Mifune (Denkicki Akama), Setsuko Hara (Taeko Nasu), Takashi Shimura (Ono), Yoshiko Kuga (Ayako, his Daughter), Chieko Higashiyama (Satoko), Chiyoko Fumiya (Noriko), Yoshiko Kuga (Ayako), Minoru Chiaki (Mutsuo Kayama), Kokuten Kodo (Jyunpei), Eiko Miyoshi (Kayama's Mother), Noriko Sengoku (Takako), Daisuke Inoue (Kaoru), Eijiro Yanagi (Tohata), Bokusen Hidari (Karube), Mitsuyo Akashi (Akama's Mother)
Distribution:	Shochiku
Running Time:	166 Minutes
Released:	May 23, 1951
U.S. Release:	April, 1963
Other Title:	L'Idiot

Synopsis

Winter. Postwar Japan. Returning to Hokkaido after a long recuperation in an army hospital, Kameda cries out, frightened by obsessive fears of being shot. A fellow passenger, Denkicki Akama laughs at the young man's idiocy. A title reads, "This is a tragic record of the ruin of a good man."

In Hokkaido the two men stare at a photograph of a famous courtesan beauty Taeko Nasu whom Akama loves and hopes to marry.

At the Kayama Inn, Taeko wearing a long black cape is the center of male attention. Currently she is the mistress of Tohata who has raised her since childhood. Kayama, a young secretary is to be paid a handsome sum by Tohata to take Taeko off his hands. Unfortunately, Kayama loves a young girl named Ayako, a relation of Kameda. Kameda is fascinated by Taeko's beauty, especially her eyes, and despite her past sees her purity.

Taeko entertains Kameda whose past suffering touches her. Kameda offers to marry and care for Taeko. Moved by this gesture, she decides not to marry Kayama and to return all that he has given her. She is tempted to accept Kameda's offer, but when she discovers he is a man of means, she refuses to ruin his life.

Akama now comes forward with the required ¥ 1,000,000 necessary to free Taeko. In a sudden fit of anger she throws the money into the fire and leaves with Akama.

Two months pass. Taeko now lives with Akama in a deserted warehouse. Kamedo visits the couple. Provoked by jealousy, Akama openly mistreats Taeko, who remains undecided between the two men. But Akama warms to Kameda despite himself and the two men have tea. Kameda's attention is drawn to a knife which lies on the stove.

Later Kameda is haunted by Akama's eyes and the image of knives. In fright he runs away, but eventually is drawn back to Akama's home. Akama pulls a knife, but finds he cannot kill Kameda. The event traumatizes Kameda.

While recovering at a relative's home, Kameda is cared for by the young Ayako. Her family wants Kameda to marry their daughter. Ayako loves him and hopes to protect him from society's cruel treatment.

One evening everyone goes for a masquerade on the ice. Taeko appears and advises Kameda to marry Ayako. A courtship begins. Kameda is quiet; Ayako often angry and jealous. Finally Kameda proposes marriage.

Still filled with jealousy, Ayako insists upon meeting Taeko, but Taeko has reservations. She considers Ayako the "soul of her dreams," the embodiment of everything she herself has lost. When Kameda brings Ayako to the warehouse the two women stare at one another in silence. Ayako blames Taeko for humiliating Kameda by deserting him. Defensive, Taeko insists that Kameda choose between the two of them. Kameda chooses Taeko. Ayako runs out, followed by Kameda. For days she languishes in bed with a high fever.

In the warehouse the two men talk. The room is dark except for one candle. Kameda discovers that Akama in a fit of madness stabbed Taeko and is keeping her dead body behind a curtain. The two men huddle under blankets through the night, slowly sinking into insanity. Outside a storm rages.

The film ends with Ayako, reassessing her life. With tears in her eyes, she blames herself. She states, "I was the idiot."

14 IKIRU, 1952

Producer:	Shojiro Motoki (Toho)
Director:	Akira Kurosawa
Photography:	Asakazu Nakai
Lighting:	Shigeru Mori

Art Direction:	So Matsuyama
Scenario:	Shinobu Hashimoto, Hideo Oguni, and Akira Kurosawa
Music:	Fumio Hayasaka
Sound:	Fumio Yanoguchi
Editor:	Koichi Iwashita
Cast:	Takashi Shimura (Kanji Watanabe, Chief, Citizens' Section), Nobuo Kaneko (Mitsuo Watanabe, his Son), Kyoko Seki (Kazue Watanabe, Mitsuo's Wife), Makoto Kobori (Kiichi Watanabe, Kanji's Elder Brother), Kumeko Urabe (Tatsu Watanabe, Kiichi's Wife), Yoshie Minami (The Maid), Miki Odagiri (Toyo Odagiri, the Girl in Watanabe's Office), Kamatari Fujiwara (Ono, Sub-section Chief), Minosuke Yamada (Saito, Subordinate Clerk), Haruo Tanaka (Sakai, Assistant), Bokuzen Hidari (Ohara, Assistant), Shinichi Himori (Kimura, Assistant), Nobuo Nakamura (Deputy Mayor), Kazuo Abe (City Assemblyman), Masao Shimizu (Doctor), Ko Kimura (Intern), Atsushi Watanabe (Patient), Yunosuke Ito (Novelist), Yatsuko Tanami (Hostess), Fuyuki Murakami (Newspaperman), Seiji Miyaguchi (Gang-boss), Daisuke Kato (Gang-member), Kin Sugai, Eiko Miyoshi, Fumiko Homma (Housewives), Ichiro Chiba (Policeman), Minoru Chiaki (Noguchi), Toranosuke Ogawa (The Park Section Chief), Tomoo Nagai, Hirayoshi Aono (Reporters), Akira Tani (Old Man at Bar), Toshiyuki Ichimura (Pianist at Cabaret)
Distribution:	Toho
Running Time:	143 Minutes
Released:	October 9, 1952
U.S. Release:	January, 1960
Other Titles:	*Living, To Live, Doomed, Vivre, Vivre enfin, un seul jour*

Synopsis

1952. A narrator announces that the man in this story, Kanji Watanabe, has stomach cancer. As chief of the Citizen's Section, Watanabe has spent his life performing menial bureaucratic duties and living a lonely, uneventful life. When a group of outraged mothers approach his office, complaining about sanitary conditions and requesting a children's playground, Watanabe disinterestedly sends them to another section and returns to his desk, piled high with papers.

Going for a medical examination Watanabe learns he has only a short time to live. In a state of shock he returns home where his son Mitsuo and daughter-in-law Kazue, involved in their own lives, have little time or patience to provide tenderness. Alienated from his son, Watanabe cannot bring himself to reveal the truth. In his own room Watanabe thinks back to his wife's funeral and the warmer days of Mitsuo's youth.

Looking for solace, Watanabe withdraws ¥ 50,000 from the bank and goes to a bar where he meets a writer. He begs the writer to show him how to have a good time, lecturing Watanabe on the knowledge of death as the liberator for enjoying life, he takes him to play pin-ball, to a beer hall, various bars and cabarets, a dance hall and strip show. In one cabaret, Watanabe, totally drunk, sings "Life Is So Short." At evening's end, he vomits in the street.

Next day on the street Watanabe meets Toyo, a former office-worker. Watanabe continues to see Toyo, enjoying her youth and zest for life. She calls him 'a mummy,' which he accepts and gradually comes to understand. Eventually, however, Toyo grows weary of Watanabe's constant attention.

At their last meeting at a fancy coffee shop, Watanabe admits that he is lonely and afraid to die. He wants to learn how to live. Toyo has no answer other than her pleasure from making toys for children. Gradually Watanabe realizes that he can take action if he really wants to.

Back at the office Watanabe hunts for the petition to reclaim the drainage area. Determined to accomplish something before he dies, Watanabe commits himself to pushing through the playground project.

Five months later. Watanabe has died. Reporters, city officials, office-workers and Watanabe's entire family gather in Watanabe's room for the funeral. The Deputy Mayor now claims credit for the park, but the reporters have uncovered contradictory evidence. The public officials support the Mayor. Only Kimura, an office-worker, defends Watanabe.

A flashback shows Watanabe's exhausting struggle to build the playground.

At the funeral a policeman arrives and describes seeing Watanabe happily singing on the children's swings the night that he died. The men at the funeral agree that Watanabe's lesson should not be lost. But next day at the office, petitions are turned away as usual. Even Kimura sits silently behind his pile of documents.

15 SEVEN SAMURAI [*Shichinin No Samurai*], 1954

Producer:	Shojiro Motoki (Toho)
Director:	Akira Kurosawa
Photography:	Asakazu Nakai
Lighting:	Shigero Mori
Art Direction:	So Matsuyama
Scenario:	Shinobu Hashimoto, Hideo Oguni, and Akira Kurosawa
Art Consultation:	Seison Maeda and Kohei Ezaki
Fencing Direction:	Yoshio Sugino
Archery Direction:	Ienori Kaneko and Shigeru Endo
Music:	Fumio Hayasaka
Sound:	Fumio Yanoguchi
Assistant Director:	Hiromichi Horikawa
Cast:	Takashi Shimura (Kambei or Kanbei Shimada, Leader of the Samurai), Toshiro Mifune (Kikuchiyo), Yoshio Inaba (Gorobei), Seiji Miyaguchi (Kyuzo), Minoru Chiaki (Heihachi), Daisuke Kato (Shichiroji), Ko Kimura (Katsushiro Okamoto), Kamatari Fujiwara (Manzo), Kuninori Kodo (Gisaku), Bokuzen Hidari (Yohei), Yoshio Kosugi (Mosuke), Yoshio Tsuchiya (Rikichi), Keiji Sakakida (Gosaku), Jiro Kumagai, Haruko Toyama, Tsuneo Katagiri, Yasuhisa Tsutsumi (Peasants), Keiko Tsushima (Shino, Manzo's Daughter), Toranosuke Ogawa (Grandfather), Yu Akitsu (Husband), Noriko Sengoku (Wife), Gen Shimizu (Masterless Samurai), Jun Tatari (Coolie), Atsushi Watanabe (Vendor), Sojin Kamiyama (Minstrel),

	Kichijiro Ueda, Shimpei Takagi, Akira Tani, Haruo Nakajima, Takashi Narita, Senkichi Omura, Shuno Takahara, Masanobu Okubo (Bandits)
Distribution:	Toho
Running Time:	160 Minutes
Released:	April 26, 1954
U.S. Release:	November, 1956
Other Titles:	*The Magnificent Seven, Les sept samouraïs*

Synopsis

The Sengoku Period. During the lawless period of civil war, bands of brigands often descended upon defenseless villages, taking food and women, and leaving the farmers impoverished. In one village a group of farmers, led by Rikichi, decide to fight back. Seeking advice from the village elder, Gisaku, they decide to hire samurai to help them defend the new barley crop.

Their first attempts lead to naught. Then, on the way to town they observe an older ronin, Kambei Shimada, rescue a kidnapped child. Impressed by his humanitarianism, strength, and intelligence, they persuade him to be their leader, although they have nothing to offer him but three meals a day.

Also watching the event are two samurai, the young Katsushiro Okamoto, who determines to follow Kambei and become his disciple, and Kikuchiyo. The ill-kempt, ill-mannered Kikuchiyo, whose claims to samurai heritage are suspicious follows the two men at a distance, loping around and carrying his long stick. In town the group search for samurai willing to take up the farmers' cause. Eventually they assemble a group of six which includes Kambei; Katsushiro; Gorobei; an intelligent ronin; Shichiroji, an old friend of Kambei's who is now out of work; Heihachi, presently employed chopping firewood; and Kyuzo, a tall, thin samurai and master swordsman. Kikuchiyo follows the six, but is not allowed into the group.

When the samurai arrive in the village, the farmers hide in fear. One farmer, Manzo, had even forced his daughter Shino to cut her hair and disguise herself as a boy. Kikuchiyo is made the seventh member of the group after sounding the village alarm, which brings the villagers out of hiding.

The next days are spent surveying the area, planning defenses, and training the villagers. In off moments Katsushiro goes into the hills where he discovers and falls in love with Shino.

Eventually three bandit scouts are spotted. They are killed by Kikuchiyo and Kyuzo while Katsushiro watches with horror. A fourth bandit is captured and brought to the village. Although he confesses and Kambei votes to spare his life, the farmers allow an old woman to avenge her son's death by killing the bandit with a three-pronged hoe.

The samurai plan a surprise attack on the bandits' fortress. Heihachi, Kyuzo, and Kikuchiyo are picked to go, taking Rikichi as their guide. The men set fire to the huts and kill the bandits as they emerge. A young woman, seeing Rikichi, runs back into the burning building. Rikichi follows, but is pulled back by Heihachi. The woman, forced into prostitution by the bandits, is Rikichi's wife. Although a shot subsequently fells Heihachi, the raid is declared a success. Back in the village Heihachi is buried and his sword placed atop the mound.

Suddenly Kikuchiyo announces that the attack is finally about to begin. Despite the coming battle, old Gisaku refuses to leave his millhouse. The bandits burn it. Kambei and Kikuchiyo go to rescue his family, but save only the child. Thirty bandits gallop toward the village, carrying three guns. A fierce battle ensues before the bandits retreat.

The samurai rest and prepare for the final attack. Again the fighting is grueling, but all the brigands are finally killed. On their side the samurai lose Gorobei, Kyuzo, and Kikuchiyo.

The fighting over, the farmers return to the fields. As Kambei leaves the village, he looks sadly at the four burial mounds and comments, "We've lost again.... The farmers are the winners."

Note

The original version of *Seven Samurai* ran 200 minutes and was shown in Japan in 1954 for a limited run only. The film was then cut for general release. A second version was made for the Venice Film Festival and another for distribution abroad. No copies of the original 200-minute print are extant. The current version available in the United States runs 151 minutes. The published screenplay (**322**), is based on the Toho script of a 160-minute version. When first shown in New York in 1956 the film was entitled *The Magnificent Seven*.

16 RECORD OF A LIVING BEING [*Ikimono No Kiroku*], 1955

Producer:	Shojiro Motoki (Toho)
Director:	Akira Kurosawa
Photography:	Asakazu Nakai
Lighting:	Kuichiro Kishida
Art Direction:	Yoshiro Muraki
Scenario:	Shinobu Hashimoto, Hideo Oguni, and Akira Kurosawa
Music:	Fumio Hayasaka — Completed by Masaru Sato
Sound:	Fumio Yanoguchi
Cast:	Toshiro Mifune (Kiichi Nakajima), Eiko Miyoshi (Toyo, his Wife), Yutaka Sada (Ichiro, his First Son), Minoru Chiaki (Jiro, his Second Son), Haruko Togo (Yoshi, his First Daughter), Kyoko Aoyama (Sué, his Second Daughter), Kiyomi Mizunoya (Kiichi's First Mistress), Saoko Yonemura (Taeko, her Daughter), Akemi Negishi (Asako, his Present Mistress), Kichijiro Ueda (Her Father), Masao Shimizu (Yamazaki, Yoshi's Husband), Noriko Sengoku (Kimie, Ichiro's Wife), Yoichi Tachikawa (Ryoichi, Nakajima's Son by a Former Mistress), Takashi Shimura (Dr. Harada, Member of the Family Court), Kazuo Kato (Susumu, his Son), Eijiro Tono (Old Man from Brazil), Ken Mitsuda (Araki, the Judge), Toranosuke Ogawa (Hori, the Lawyer), Kamatari Fujiwara (Okamoto), Nobuo Nakamura (Psychiatrist)
Distribution:	Toho
Running Time:	113 Minutes

Released: November 22, 1955
U.S. Release: January, 1967
Other Titles: *I Live in Fear, What the Birds Knew, Chronique d'un être vivant, Vivre dans la peur, Notes d'un être vivant, Si les oiseaux saviaent*

Synopsis

1955. Dr. Harada, a Tokyo dentist, serves as a volunteer mediator in Family Court. His present case involves a successful foundry owner, Kiichi Nakijima, whose family want him declared incompetent. Nakijima is obsessed by the danger of radioactive fallout in Japan and believes that South America is the only safe place left in the world. Harada is fascinated by the case and is sympathetic to Nakijima's concern.

Nakijima has begun negotiations with a Japanese farmer who owns land in Brazil. He hopes to move his entire family, including mistresses and their children, there. At home, startled by the sounds of planes and a sudden summer storm, he grows increasingly hysterical.

Harada questions the Nakijima family about moving, but learns that none of them can conceive of life away from Japan and the foundry, although Nakijima's wife is willing to do whatever will make her husband happy. The family fears that Nakijima will sell the foundry and impoverish them all. Harada continues to study the case, reading material on the effect of atomic explosion.

The farmer needs money to purchase land in Japan. Nakijima borrows funds from his mistress and his sons, but eventually returns the money since the court has forbidden him to carry out business transactions.

The court finally decides in favor of the family. Harada meets Nakijima by accident on a train. At first Nakijima refuses to talk to him. Then Nakijima tells him that initially he was moved by reason, but now reacts through fear. He says life has become a living inferno. He blames Harada for his condition.

At home Nakijima, still convinced of the urgency of his cause, pleads with his family to leave. Sick with exhaustion, he faints and is taken to bed.

Harada pays a visit to the foundry. As he approaches he sees that the whole building is now reduced to ashes. The son reprimands an employee, but Nakijima admits that he set the building aflame to force his family to leave Japan. Suddenly jobless, the employees turn against him in anger. Nakijima realizes he has been selfish. The police arrive and Nakijima is taken to jail.

When Harada comes to pay a final visit, Nakijima is lost in his own world. Completely broken, he now leaves at an asylum. Looking through his window, Nakijima sees the sun and suddenly grows fearful, believing the earth is burning up. Disheartened Harada leaves.

17 THE THRONE OF BLOOD [*Kumonosu-Jo*], 1957

Producers: Shojiro Motoki and Akira Kurosawa (Toho)
Director: Akira Kurosawa
Screenplay: Shinobu Hashimoto, Ryuzo Kikushima, Hideo Oguni and Akira Kurosawa, Based on William Shakespeare's Drama *Macbeth*

Photography:	Asakazu Nakai
Art Direction:	Yoshiro Muraki and Kohei Ezaki
Scenario:	Shinobu Hashimoto, Ryuzo Kikushima, Hideo Oguni, and Akira Kurosawa
Music:	Masaru Sato
Sound:	Fumio Yanoguchi
Cast:	Toshiro Mifune (Taketoki Washizu), Isuzu Yamada (Asaji, his Wife), Minoru Chiaki (Yoshiaki Miki, his Friend), Akira Kubo (Yoshiteru, Miki's Son), Takamaru Sasaki (Kuniharu Tsuzuki), Yoichi Tachikawa (Kunimaru, Kuniharu's Son), Takashi Shimura (Noriyasu Odagura), Chieko Naniwa (Witch)
Distribution:	Toho
Running Time:	110 Minutes
Released:	January 15, 1957
U.S. Release:	November, 1961
Other Titles:	*The Castle of the Spider's Web, Cobweb Castle, Kunonosu-Djo, Le chateau l'ariagnée, Le trône sanglant, Macbeth*

Synopsis

Medieval Japan. Partially hidden in the fog, a post stone appears while the narrator states that this marks the ruins of a once invincible fortress.

On a low, windy plain a messenger arrives at the Castle of the Spider's Web to announce the victory of Captain Taketoki Washizu over the rebellious armies. Returning home from battle amidst rain and fog, Washizu and his comrade Yoshiaki Miki pass through a forest. They stumble upon an old, white-haired hag who sings of pride and death and prophesies Washizu's rise to power, but lasting rule for Miki's descendants. At home the two men are duly honored by his lordship and raised to the rank of general.

In their private compartments, Lady Washizu rouses her husband's ambitions and turns his jealousy against Miki. Together they plot to kill his Lordship Kuniharu. After drugging the guards, Lady Washizu fills her husband with courage. Washizu returns, bloody and dazed, having completed the murder. Lady Washizu plants the necessary evidence and washes the blood from her hands, while Washizu yells "murder" and kills the sleeping guards. The household is roused to a state of panic.

A stately funeral follows outside the castle walls. The women weep for her Ladyship, who committed suicide. Washizu plans to name Miki his successor, but Lady Washizu announces her pregnancy.

On the evening of a grand banquet, Miki's horse returns riderless. The kyogen players perform a dance about an ambitious man. Agitated, Washizu stops the performance. Guilt-ridden, he sees Miki's ghost seated at the table. After the guests leave, a soldier enters with Miki's head. In a fit of rage Washizu slays him.

Time goes by, bringing more murders. In the windy courtyard, the men discuss recent events and the oppression of evil days. One says that even the rats are deserting the house. Lady Washizu delivers a stillborn child and hovers between life and death.

Beyond the castle, Miki's son is gathering an army to prepare an attack. Ill-at-ease Washizu rides out in the rain to find the witch once more. She tells him he is safe until the forest moves to the castle. Escaping from the ghosts of previous victims, Washizu returns home.

At the castle Washizu tries to instill courage in his men. Standing on a parapet he looks for the unseen enemy which can be heard in the forest. Suddenly a swarm of birds descend upon the castle. The men panic. Washizu visits his wife, who is now lost in madness. Outside Miki's army, camouflaged with tree branches, moves toward the fortress. No longer responsive to his command, Washizu's soldiers turn on him with a rain of arrows. Finally one pierces his neck. Slowly he sinks and dies. Miki's son approaches and takes command of the castle.

Once again the post stone appears and the fog closes in.

18 THE LOWER DEPTHS [*Donzoko*], 1957

Producers:	Shojiro Motoki and Akira Kurosawa (Toho)
Director:	Akira Kurosawa
Screenplay:	Hideo Oguni and Akira Kurosawa, Based on Maxim Gorky's Drama *The Lower Depths*
Photography:	Kazuo Yamasaki
Art Direction:	Yoshiro Muraki
Scenario:	Hideo Oguni and Akira Kurosawa
Music:	Masaru Sato
Cast:	Toshiro Mifune (Sutekichi, the Thief), Isuzu Yamada (Osugi, Landlady), Ganjiro Nakamura (Rokubei, her Husband), Kyoko Kagawa (Okayo, her Sister), Bokuzen Hidari (Kahei, Priest), Minoru Chiaki (Ex-Samurai), Kamatari Fujiwara (Actor), Eijiro Tono (Tomekichi, Tinker), Eiko Miyoshi (Asa, his Wife), Akemi Negishi (Osen, Prostitute), Koji Mitsui (Yoshisaburo, Gambler), Nijiko Kiyokawa (Otaki), Haruo Tanaka (Tatsu), Kichijiro Ueda (Police Agent)
Distribution:	Toho
Running Time:	137 Minutes
Released:	September 17, 1957
U.S. Release:	February, 1962
Other Title:	*Les bas-fonds*

Synopsis

Edo period. A temple gong sounds. Villagers throw garbage over the hillside. Down in the pit Yoshisaburo, a gambler, cynically comments on the life around him.

Existing amidst poverty and dirt, in a hovel where the ceiling constantly leaks rain, a group of lost souls go about their daily business. The group includes: The landlord, Rokubei, a miserly, henpecked husband; his greedy wife, Osugi, who callously dominates all those around her; her sister, Okayo; a thief, Sutekichi, who loves Okayo; a tinker, Tomekichi, who aspires to be a craftsman; his wife, Asa, who is dying of tuberculosis; a prostitute, Osen, who daydreams of her one great love; an alcoholic actor, who can no longer remember his lines; an ex-samurai who lives on past glories; and a pilgrim priest, Kahei, who inspires the others with hope.

Among themselves they fight as each tries to eke out a better existence. Sutekichi steals from the others and turns over his proceeds to Rokubei, who rewards him with a room of his own. Osugi lusts after Sutekichi and tries to convince him to kill her husband, but Sutekichi is only interested in Okayo, who does not return his love. Eventually Sutekichi and Rokubei confront one another. Sutekichi comes close to killing Rokubei, but is distracted by the priest.

Asa dies, comforted only by the kind words of the priest. After much effort, the actor remembers his lines. Osen again tells the story of her great love while the others laugh at her reveries.

Sutekichi begs Okayo to run away with him, but she does not trust him. The priest comments on the universal need to be loved. Osugi, jealous of Sutekichi's attentions, throws boiling water at her sister. Sutekichi and Rokubei join the altercation. Sutekichi pushes too hard and Rokubei is killed. Sobbing hysterically, Okayo denounces him to the police.

Time has passed. The group talk about the great event. Osen has since gone mad. Okayo has married a former police runner and daily grows more like her sister. The actor, although reformed, takes a drink and goes outside. The ex-samurai questions what will become of them. The men drink saké and gradually break into song and dance. The merriment is cut short, however, by the samurai's announcement that the actor has hanged himself. Cynical as always, Yoshisaburo remarks, "He spoiled our fun."

19 THE HIDDEN FORTRESS [*Kakushi Toride No San-Akunin*], 1958

Producers:	Masumi Fujimoto and Akira Kurosawa (Toho)
Director:	Akira Kurosawa
Photography:	Kazuo Yamasaki
Lighting:	Ichiro Inohara
Art Direction:	Yoshiro Muraki and Kohei Ezaki
Scenario:	Shinobu Hashimoto, Ryuzo Kikushima, Hideo Oguni, and Akira Kurosawa
Music:	Masaru Sato
Sound:	Fumio Yanoguchi
Cast:	Toshiro Mifune (General Rokurota Makabe), Misa Uehara (Princess Yukihime), Takashi Shimura (General Izumi Nagakura), Susumu Fujita (General Hyoe Tadokoro), Eiko Miyoshi (Lady-in-Waiting), Minoru Chiaki (Tahei), Kamatari Fujiwara (Matashichi or Matakishi), Toshiko Higuchi (Girl), Kichijiro Ueda (Slaver), Koji Mitsui (Soldier), Rinsaku Ogata (Young Man), Tadao Nakamaru (Young Man), Ikio Sawamura (Gambling Man), Shiten Ohashi (Samurai Buying a Horse), Kokuten Kodo (Man at the Signboard), Takeshi Kato (Stray Soldier), Yoshio Kosugi, Haruo Nakajima, Senkichi Omura (Akisuki Soldiers), Shoichi Hirose (Yamana Soldier), Toranosuke Ogawa (Warrior), Yutaka

The Films: Synopsis, Credits and Notes / 57

Sada (Guard at Barrier Gate), Shin Otomo (Mounted Samurai), Yutaka Nakayama, Makoto Sato, Jiro Kumagai (Foot Soldiers), Etsuro Saijyo (Stray Soldier), Akira Tani, Sachio Sakai (Foot Soldiers Catching Rokurota), Takeo Oikawa, Yu Fujiki (Soldiers at the Checking Station), Yoshio Tsuchiya (Mounted Samurai of Hayakawa)

Distribution: Toho
Running Time: 139 Minutes
Format: Tohoscope
Released: December 28, 1958
U.S. Release: January, 1962
Other Titles: *Three Bad Men in a Hidden Fortress, Trois salauds dans une forteresse cachée, La forteresse cachée*

Synopsis

Amidst the chaos of the 16th century civil wars, two farmers, Tahei and Matashichi, walk along complaining and quarreling. When bandits appear, they are pressed into service, digging for hidden gold. Falling fire causes sudden panic and the two escape during the commotion.

Accidentally Tahei and Matashichi find gold hidden in bamboo shoots. As they scramble for more among the rocks, they are stopped in their tracks by the imposing figure of Rokurota, who towers over them, legs astride. Rokurota leads them to a hidden fortress where he takes their gold and puts them to work.

At a pond they meet a young girl dressed in boy's clothes. Unaware that she is really the lady Yukihime, temporarily in disguise, they give chase until both are stopped by Rokurota, who discloses Yukihime's part of the truth. When the two men discover Yukihime's comb, they run to town to claim a reward. Unhappily they are informed of the princess' execution the preceding day.

Apart from the rest of the group, against the sound of trumpets, Rokurota pays homage to the princess. As her general he has sacrificed his sister, also age sixteen, who was executed in her place to save the royal house.

The group prepares to make their way through enemy territory. The gold is placed in firewood and loaded onto horses. Yukihime is disguised as a deaf serving girl. Rokurota counts on the greed of the two farmers to insure their loyalty. However, the men do attempt to desert, breaking into dance-like movements as they attempt to cross a river. In town the group deceive the guard and spend the night at a local inn. Yukihime, incensed at the treatment of several women, buys them and sets them free.

Next day on the road the group is recognized. Rokurota kills several soldiers, but mistakenly charges into the enemy camp. Challenged to a duel by General Hyoe Tadokoro, the two men fight with lances until Rokurota defeats Tadokoro. Sparing his life, Rokurota rides off leaving Tadokoro alive, but in shame.

That evening the group watch the Yamana Fire Festival. The celebrants grow wilder as all engage in song and dance. The festivities are interrupted, however, by the approaching enemy army. The servants rush to protect Yuki and all escape. Tahei and Matashichi take advantage of this opportunity to again defect.

When the group are within sight of freedom, they are arrested and taken to prison. General Tadokoro appears, still bitter after his public humiliation. Princess Yukihime announces her willingness to die having tasted the fullness of life. She sings the fire-festival song.

With an unexpected change of heart, Tadokoro releases the couple, fights against his own men, and finally defects himself. From the mountain top they spy the two farmers, with the gold-laden horses, still quarreling. Friendly soldiers arrive with banners. In safety Princess Yukihime and Rokurota appear in royal robes and full armor against a background of drums and tambourines. The captured farmers are brought before them, forgiven, and sent home with thanks and a single piece of gold.

20 THE BAD SLEEP WELL [*Warui Yatsu Hodo Yoku Nemuru*], 1960

Producer:	Tomoyuki Tanaka and Akira Kurosawa (Kurosawa Films Production/Toho)
Director:	Akira Kurosawa
Photography:	Yuzuru Aizawa
Lighting:	Ichiro Inohara
Art Direction:	Yoshiro Muraki
Scenario:	Shinobu Hashimoto, Hideo Oguni, Ryuzo Kikushima, Eijiro Hisaita, and Akira Kurosawa
Music:	Masaru Sato
Sound:	Fumio Yanoguchi and Hisashi Shimogawa
Cast:	Toshiro Mifune (Koichi Nishi, Secretary to Iwabuchi), Takeshi Kato (Itakura, his Friend), Masayuki Mori (Iwabuchi, the President), Takashi Shimura (Moriyama, Administrative Officer), Akira Nishimura (Shirai, Contract Officer), Kamatari Fujiwara (Wada, Accountant), Gen Shimizu (Miura, Accountant), Kyoko Kagawa (Keiko or Yoshio, Iwabuchi's Daughter), Tatsuya Mihashi (Tatsuo, Iwabuchi's Son), Kyu Sazanka (Kaneko), Chishu Ryu (Nonaka, Public Prosecutor), Seiji Miyaguchi (Okakura), Nobuo Nakamura (Lawyer), Susumu Fujita (Commissioner), Koji Mitsui (Journalist), Ken Mitsuda (Arimura), Sensho Matsumoto (Hatano), Kin Sugai (Tomoko Wada), Toshiko Higuchi (Masako Wada), Koji Nanbara (Horiuchi), Yoshio Tsuchiya (A.D.A. Secretary), Kunie Tanaka (Professional Killer), Hiromi Mineoka (Maid), Natsuko Kahara (Furuya's Wife), Yoshibumi Tajima (Reporter), Hisashi Yokomori (Reporter), Yutaka Sada (Receptionist), Ikio Sawamura (Driver)
Distribution:	Toho
Running Time:	151 Minutes
Format:	Tohoscope
Released:	September 4, 1960
U.S. Release:	January, 1963
Other Titles:	*The Worse You Are the Better You Sleep, The Rose in the Mud, Les salauds dorment en paix, Les salauds se portent bien*

Synopsis

1961. At a modern Tokyo hotel wedding ceremonies begin for Keiko, the daughter of a powerful corporation president and her father's secretary, Koichi Nishi. The press are shocked to discover Keiko is lame. While formal speeches are delivered the reporters comment on the various principles and talk of predicted scandals. The banquet is interrupted by the arrest of Wada, the company accountant, but continues as Tatsuo, Keiko's brother, delivers a passionate speech warning Nishi to be good to his sister. The wedding cake arrives, followed by another in the shape of an office building. This is placed in front of President Iwabuchi who appears visibly agitated. The building is a reminder of an old scandal involving a suicide fall of a company official.

A montage sequence covering the succeeding weeks details newspaper headlines of arrests and bribery. Miura, a corporation official, is sent to Tokyo Prison. Bowing to company pressure, he throws himself in front of an automobile.

Atop a hill on the outskirts of Tokyo, Wada is about to throw himself into the pit below when Nishi stops him. Nishi persuades Wada that he is a fool to die for the bosses.

Believing Wada dead, Iwabuchi arranges an appropriate funeral. Nishi forces Wada to watch his own funeral and to listen to a tape recording of the bosses callously planning his death. Shaken, Wada breaks down and agrees to help Nishi and his friend, a man whose name Nishi has borrowed to disguise his real identity. Nishi is obsessed by a desire to destroy Iwabuchi and his corrupt cohorts.

The company officials are disturbed by the theft of ¥ 5,000,000. Immediately Shirai, a contract officer, is suspected. Nishi has planted the money in his briefcase. To further intimidate Shirai, Wada appears and disappears like a ghost as Shirai makes his way home along dark streets.

At home Nishi and his wife sleep in separate bedrooms. Gradually, however, Nishi finds himself drawn to Keiko despite his ulterior motives in marrying her.

At a family gathering Iwabuchi, wearing an apron, cooks dinner. However, Tatsuo is not deceived by such kindly gestures and tells Nishi that his father is "a bad man."

Shirai shows signs of cracking. Iwabuchi and his assistant Moriyama decide to dispose of him. As an armed assassin approaches Shirai one evening, Nishi drives past and saves him. But Nishi has saved Shirai to inflict his own revenge. Nishi holds Shirai responsible for his father's suicidal jump from the Tokyo building five years before. Showing no pity he drags Shirai to a downtown office. First he threatens to push Shirai off a window ledge and then he pours poison (in reality whiskey) down his throat. Wada, frightened and appalled by such behavior, calls Nishi "a terrible man." Next day Shirai is found alive and committed to a hospital.

Meanwhile Moriyama does some investigating and discovers the truth. When Tatsuo overhears a conversation with his father, he threatens to kill Nishi who ironically has just decided to abandon the plot and consummate his marriage. Later Nishi telephones to say he and his accomplice have kidnapped Moriyama.

The two men hold Moriyama in an abandoned air-raid shelter, without food. Wada wants to relent, but Nishi says such conduct only keeps the wicked strong. Wada runs off and returns with Nishi's wife. Her coming indicates her love for Nishi, but she is unable to hate her own father.

At home Iwabuchi receives a telephone call from his superior and prepares to take sleeping medicine, but Keiko returns home and he drugs her and obtains the necessary information.

At the air-raid shelter Moriyama finally confesses, but Nishi's success comes too late. When Tatsuo and Keiko arrive they learn from the real Nishi that Iwabuchi has had Nishi and Wada killed in what looks like a drunken automobile accident and that Moriyama has already destroyed all the evidence.

Returning home the two renounce their father and leave. As they exit, Iwabuchi receives a telephone call from his superior. Apologizing profusely, he offers his resignation.

Note

The Bad Sleep Well was Kurosawa's first film for Kurosawa Productions, an independent producing unit run and financed by Kurosawa and partially underwritten by Toho. The Japanese version runs 151 minutes, but was cut to 135 for foreign release.

21 YOJIMBO, 1961

Producers:	Tomoyuki Tanaka and Ryuzo Kikushima (Kurosawa Films Production/Toho)
Director:	Akira Kurosawa
Photography:	Kazuo Miyagawa
Lighting:	Choshiro Ishii
Art Direction:	Yoshiro Muraki
Scenario:	Ryuzo Kikushima and Akira Kurosawa
Music:	Masaru Sato
Sound:	Hisashi Shimonaga and Choshichiro Mikami
Cast:	Toshiro Mifune (Sanjuro Kuwabatake), Eijiro Tono (Gonji, the Saké-seller), Kamatari Fujiwara (Tazaemon, the Silk Merchant), Takashi Shimura (Tokuemon, the Saké Merchant), Seizaburo Kawazu (Seibei, Tazaemon's Henchman), Isuzu Yamada (Orin, Seibei's Wife), Hiroshi Tachikawa (Yoichiro, their Son), Kyu Sazanka (Ushitora, Tokuemon's Henchman), Tatsuya Nakadai (Unosuke, Ushitora's Younger Brother), Daisuke Kato (Inokichi, Ushitora's Brother), Ikio Sawamura (Hansuke), Akira Nishimura (Kuma), Yoshio Tsuchiya (Kohei, a Farmer), Yoko Tsukasa (Nui, his Wife), Susumu Fujita (Homma, the Ex-yojimbo)
Distribution:	Toho
Running Time:	110 Minutes
Format:	TohoScope
Released:	April 25, 1961
U.S. Release:	October, 1962
Other Titles:	The Bodyguard, Le garde du corps

Synopsis

Unable to find employment in the closing years of the Tokugawa Period, Sanjuro Kuwabatake, a masterless samurai, tosses a stick in the air and goes off in the direction it leads. Swaggering and munching on a toothpick, he comes upon a dusty town desolated by warring factions and violence. He is greeted by a dog carrying a severed hand. The menfolk, ugly and maimed, emerge from shuttered houses and look him over, all the while bragging about their prowess.

After learning the town history, Sanjuro sizes up the situation. Seeing an opportunity to earn some money by playing one group off against the other, he takes a job as bodyguard (yojimbo) to Tazaemon, the silk merchant and his henchman Ushitora. Secretively he plans to rid the town of both evil forces.

Taunting the men with cowardliness, Sanjuro attacks several ruffians and then crosses over to the opposing faction. Hiring himself to Tokuemon, the saké merchant, and his henchman, Seibei, he spirals his salary from three to fifty ryo. In a private conversation with his wife and son, Seibei reveals his plan to kill Sanjuro after they have utilized his services. Not long afterwards Sanjuro leaves Tokuemon as well.

The two groups meet in the street, each creating noise to disguise their own fears. Sanjuro sits aloft on a firetower to observe their folly. The fight is interrupted, however, by the arrival of an inspector. All activity stops when the rains come. Then Ushitora arrives with a giant-sized ruffian. Temporarily the two groups make peace.

The truce lasts until Ushitora's younger brother, Unosuke, arrives. More sadistic and sophisticated than the rest, he possesses a gun, which he fires into the air as an indication of his power.

Sanjuro goes to Seibei's house where geisha girls perform dances and play instruments. He is kidnapped, severely beaten and kept in confinement. With great effort Sanjuro manages to escape and hide in a barrel-shaped coffin. Meanwhile the fighting continues and more villains are killed.

Unwittingly, Inokichi carries the concealed Sanjuro to the cemetery. Sanjuro rises from the coffin battered and weak. Fleeing to a nearby temple, he recovers and plots new tactics.

The town is now more desolate and devastated than ever. The final battle is ready to begin. Sanjuro confronts Unosuke and knifes him before he can fire a fatal shot. Sanjuro releases the innocent saké-seller who has been hanging from a rope and angrily slaughters many of the remaining villains. Unosuke requests his now empty pistol. Sanjuro complies, only to learn it is a trick. Unosuke tries to kill Sanjuro with his one remaining bullet, but blacks out and the bullet goes astray. A watchman emerges banging his drums, and Sanjuro, having accomplished his business, strides out of town.

22 SANJURO, 1962

Producers:	Tomoyuki Tanaka and Ryuzo Kikushima (Kurosawa Films Production/Toho)
Director:	Akira Kurosawa

Screenplay: Based on the novel *Tsubaki Sanjuro* by Shugoro Yamamoto
Photography: Fukuzo Koizumi
Lighting: Ichiro Inohara
Art Direction: Yoshiro Muraki
Scenario: Ryuzo Kikushima, Hideo Oguni, and Akira Kurosawa
Music: Masaru Sato
Sound: Wataru Konuma and Hisashi Shimonaga
Adviser on
  Swordplay: Ryu Kuze
Cast: Toshiro Mifune (Sanjuro Tsubaki), Tatsuya Nakadai (Hanbei Muroto), Yuzo Kayama (Iiro Izaka, Leader of the Samurai), Akihiko Hirata, Kunie Tanaka, Hiroshi Tachikawa, Tatsuhiko Hari, Tatsuyoshi Ehara, Kenzo Matsui, Yoshio Tsuchiya, Akira Kubo (Samurai), Takashi Shimura (Kurofuji), Kamatari Fujiwara (Takebayashi), Masao Shimizu (Inspector Kikui), Yunosuke Ito (Chamberlain Mutsuta, Iiro's Uncle), Takako Irie (His Wife), Reiko Dan (Chidori, his Daughter), Keiju Kobayashi (The Spy)
Distribution: Toho
Running Time: 96 Minutes
Format: TohoScope
Released: January 1, 1962
U.S. Release: May, 1963

Synopsis

Japan. Tokugawa Period. Nine young, inexperienced samurai headed by Iiro Izaka gather together to find a means of ending corruption in the clan. Warned by Iiro's uncle, Chamberlain Mutsuta, that things are not always what they seem and that they best mind their own affairs, the group has put their trust in Inspector Kikui. Unexpectedly, out of the darkness emerges a disheveled samurai, Sanjuro Tsubaki, scratching himself and offering advice. Sanjuro believes that Inspector Kikui is the unseen danger and warns them not to be deceived by appearances.

So said, the group suddenly realizes that the house is surrounded by Kikui's men. Sanjuro emerges and single-handedly wards off the enemy led by Hanbei Muroto, while the young men hide under the floor. Bowing to Sanjuro's superior skill and knowledge, the young men offer thanks for their lives.

The group, which now includes Sanjuro, plans to rescue Iiro's uncle and his family, who are now Kikui's prisoners. At Mutsuta's home, they succeed in rescuing the women, but the uncle has already been taken elsewhere. They rest momentarily in a barn where Sanjuro plans to kill a captured guard spy. Mutsuta's wife objects to such violence, lecturing Sanjuro that "The best sword stays in its scabbard." Deferring to her authority, the group escapes over the wall with their prisoner.

Each side now makes its own plans. The chamberlain refuses to talk and the enemy decides to deploy a decoy. They send out an empty palanquin in order to draw their opponents. The young samurai discover the trick and report back to Sanjuro.

Sanjuro, on a spy mission, offers himself to Muroto. Still apprehensive about Sanjuro's true allegiance, the young men follow him and are captured. To save their lives Sanjuro must emulate an enemy attack and kill all of Muroto's guards. The wasteful spilling of so much blood incenses him. The samurai bind Sanjuro in ropes and flee. Muroto finds him and dismisses him from service.

Meanwhile, next door, Chidori, the chamberlain's daughter, finds a note from her father in a stream which flows from Camilla Mansion. Assured of Mutsuta's whereabouts, the group now plans an attack. Sanjuro wants to burn Camilla Mansion as a signal for the attack, but Mutsuta's wife suggests sending camellias down stream instead. Sanjuro then goes once more to fight for Muroto.

Muroto accepts him back, but then suspicious, ties him up. However, Sanjuro is able to trick his guards into shaking flowers into the stream. The signal arrives; the samurai attack; and the chamberlain returns home safely.

At the formal dinner celebrating Mutsuta's return, Sanjuro fails to appear. Aware that his usefulness has past, he is already on the road. Iiro and his friends run after him, and Muroto, still unsatisfied, challenges him to a duel unto death. The two stand facing one another for many moments, then simultaneously draw. Sanjuro's sword is surer. Muroto spouts blood and dies. Warning the young samurai not to be a "drawn sword," Sanjuro goes off down the road.

23 HIGH AND LOW [Tengoku To Jigoku], 1963

Producers:	Tomoyuki Tanaka and Ryuzo Kikushima (Kurosawa Films Production/Toho)
Director:	Akira Kurosawa
Screenplay:	Ryuzo Kikushima, Hideo Oguni, and Akira Kurosawa, Based on Ed McBain's Novel *King's Ransom*
Photography:	Asakazu Nakai
Lighting:	Ichiro Inohara
Art Direction:	Yoshiro Muraki
Scenario:	Ryuzo Kikushima, Hideo Oguni, and Akira Kurosawa
Music:	Masaru Sato
Sound:	Hisahi Shimonaga
Cast:	Toshiro Mifune (Kingo Gondo), Kyoko Kagawa (Reiko, his Wife), Tatsuya Mihashi (Kawanishi, her Brother), Yutaka Sada (Aoki, the Chauffeur), Tatsuya Nakadai (Inspector Tokuro), Takashi Shimura (Director), Susumu Fujita (Commissioner), Kenjiro Ishiyama (Detective Taguchi), Ko Kimura (Detective Arai), Takeshi Kato (Detective Nakao), Yoshio Tsuchiyama (Detective Murata), Hiroshi Unayama (Detective Shimada), Koji Mitsui (Newspaperman), Tsutomu Yamazaki (Ginji Takeuchi or Saganuchi, the Kidnapper)
Distribution:	Toho
Running Time:	143 Minutes
Format:	TohoScope

Released: March 1, 1963
U.S. Release: November, 1963
Other Titles: *Heaven and Hell, The Ransom, Le paradis et l'enfer, Entre le ciel et l'enfer*

Synopsis

Yokohama. 1962. During a business meeting at his home high above the city Kingo Gondo, President of the National Shoe Company, defends his policy of manufacturing the finest product on the market. In order to gain company control, Gondo has mortgaged his house and possessions to raise ¥ 50,000,000. His plan is jeopardized when a kidnapper telephones, demanding ¥ 30,000 or the life of Gondo's son. It soon becomes apparent, however, that the kidnapper has taken the chauffeur's son by mistake.

Despite the kidnapper's warning, Gondo informs the police. Aoki, the chauffeur, breaks down after hearing a tape recording of his son and begs Gondo to pay the money. Gondo refuses.

Inspector Tokuro convinces Gondo to pay the ransom in order to save the child and obtain information which may lead to an arrest and hopefully to the recovery of Gondo's money.

Plans are arranged. Gondo will carry a money-filled briefcase onto a train. When he sees the boy along the route he will throw the case out the bathroom window. Before Gondo leaves, however, he and the police prepare the briefcase with a special chemical which will produce pink smoke when burned.

All goes as planned and the boy is recovered. The police now mobilize and the investigation begins in earnest. In a poor section of the city, Ginji Takeuchi, the kidnapper, listens to a radio broadcast of public sympathy for Gondo. From a film taken on the train the police determine that the kidnapper had two accomplices. Further details are obtained from questioning the child and from his drawing.

Various trails lead to a house where the police find the two accomplices, dead from an overdose of heroin. The police ask the press to withhold this information for the present to confuse Takeuchi.

A newspaper article picturing the missing briefcase causes Takeuchi to burn the evidence. The appearance of pink smoke brings the police, who discover Takeuchi's identity. Facts lead to a city hospital where Takeuchi works as an intern. The police decide against an immediate arrest in hopes of proving a murder charge as well as kidnapping.

A false note is sent to Takeuchi, supposedly from the accomplices. Meanwhile the police tail him through the seedy streets and bars of Yokohama where he purchases heroin. To test the potency of the drug Takeuchi overdoses a young whore in a deserted harbor building, thus killing a third victim.

Takeuchi then returns to the house where he is arrested. All but ¥ 20,000 (which Takeuchi spent on heroin) is recovered, although it is too late to save Gondo's position.

Two weeks later, days before Takeuchi's execution, Gondo goes to the prison. Gondo has now started again in a small shoe business. Takeuchi, who has requested to see Gondo, wants to prove he is not afraid to die. Separated by a glass screen, the two men confront one another.

24 RED BEARD [Akahige], 1965

Producers:	Ryuzo Kikushima and Tomoyuki Tanaka (Kurosawa Films Production/Toho)
Director:	Akira Kurosawa
Screenplay:	Ryuzo Kikushima, Hideo Oguni, Masato Ide, and Akira Kurosawa, Based on the Novel *Akahige* by Shugoro Yamamoto
Photography:	Asakazu Nakai and Takao Saito
Lighting:	Hiromitsu Mori
Art Direction:	Yoshiro Muraki
Scenario:	Ryuzo Kikushima, Hideo Oguni, Masato Ide, and Akira Kurosawa
Music:	Masaru Sato
Sound:	Shin Watarai
Cast:	Toshiro Mifune (Dr. Kyojio Niide [Akahige]), Yuzo Kayama (Dr. Noboru Yasumoto), Yoshio Tsuchiya (Dr. Handayu Mori), Tatsuyoshi Ehara (Genzo Tsugawa), Reiko Dan (Osugi), Kyoko Kagawa (The Mad Woman), Kamatari Fujiwara (Rokusuke), Akemi Negishi (Okuni), Tsutomu Yamazaki (Sahachi), Miyuki Kuwano (Onaka), Eijiro Tono (Goheiji), Takashi Shimura (Tokubei Izumiya), Terumi Niki (Otoyo), Haruko Sugimura (Kin), Yoko Naito (Masae), Ken Mitsuda (Her Father), Kinuyo Tanaka (Noboru's Mother), Chishu Ryu (Noboru's Father), Yoshitaka Zushi (Choji)
Distribution:	Toho
Running Time:	185 Minutes
Format:	TohoScope
Sound:	Four-track Stereophonic
Released:	April 3, 1965
U.S. Release:	December, 1968
Other Title:	*Barbe rouge, Barberousse*

Synopsis

Edo. Late Tokugawa Period. Dr. Noboru Yasumoto, an outstanding recent graduate, arrives at the Koishikawa Public Clinic to begin his internship. He is warned by a leaving physician of the terrible conditions which prevail and of the tyrannical rule of Red Beard (Dr. Niide). However, others, including Dr. Mori and many of the patients, hold a differing view of the formidable chief.

Yasumoto meets with Red Beard and voices his bitterness about not being assigned to the Shogunate's service as he had expected. Determined to win his discharge by disobeying the rules, Yasumoto enters forbidden areas of the hospital, refuses to eat or to share his medical notes with Red Beard, and to wear a medical uniform. Arrogantly he claims to know more than Red Beard.

Alone in his room Yasumoto sees a beautiful, but crazed, young woman at his doorway. She has escaped from her nurse, Osugi. Pleading for help, she enters and tells Yasumoto about several childhood sexual assaults. As Yasumoto tries to calm her, she wraps him in her obi and attempts to stab him with a hair pin. He is saved by Red Beard's arrival, luckily escaping with only a neck graze.

After his recovery Red Beard calls him to attend to a dying man. He is appalled by the horror and agony of the scene and is shocked to hear Red Beard reassure the man's daughter that her father died in peace. Red Beard explains that with all of life's suffering, one should not have to face such an ultimate injustice. Later Yasumoto assists Red Beard during an operation. Unable to cope with the harsh realities, he faints.

Yasumoto sits for awhile with Sahachi, a favorite patient, now living out his last days. Sahachi tells Yasumoto he should wear his uniform because it gives confidence to the patients. Told through the use of flashbacks, Sahachi relates his life and tragic love for a young girl Onaka, explaining how he came to dedicate his life to serving others. After Sahachi's death, Yasumoto dons a uniform.

During a medical visit at a brothel, Red Beard finds the madam abusing a twelve-year old girl, Otoyo. Transfixed, Otoyo compulsively scrubs the floor. To gain possession of the child, Red Beard fights several of the madam's strong men, leaving Yasumoto to mend their broken bones.

At the clinic he gives Otoyo to Yasumoto as his first patient. Initially, she refuses to talk or to take her medicine, but slowly Yasumoto gains her confidence and cures her.

Yasumoto learns that he had been assigned to the clinic to hasten his recovery from a broken romance. Overworked, Yasumoto becomes ill. Otoyo gently nurses him back to health and falls in love. She is extremely jealous of the aristocratic Masae, the sister of Yasumoto's ex-fiancée. Gradually, however, Otoyo turns her attention to others. She allows a young beggar boy called "the rat" to steal rice, but at the same time tries to persuade him to beg instead of stealing.

Yasumoto receives a request from the Shogun's doctor to join his staff, but Yasumoto now wants to remain at the clinic and implement the teachings of Red Beard. An emergency brings the doctors to "little rat's" house. Unable to stay alive, the whole family has taken poison. The women yell down a well to recall his soul. Happily, the doctors are able to save him, the one member of the family to survive.

Yasumoto is betrothed to Masae in a formal ceremony and Red Beard agrees to take Yasumoto on as a clinic doctor.

25 DODESKADEN [*Dodesukaden*], 1970

Producers:	Akira Kurosawa, Keisuke Kinoshita, Kon Ichikawa, Masaki Kobayashi (Yonki no Kai/Toho)
Executive Producer:	Akira Kurosawa
Director:	Akira Kurosawa
Screenplay:	Akira Kurosawa, Hideo Oguni, and Shinobu Hashimoto, Based on Shugoro Yamamoto's Novel *The Town Without Seasons*
Photography:	Takao Saito and Yasumichi Fukuzawa
Art Direction:	Yoshiro and Shinobu Muraki
Music:	Toru Takemitsu
Sound:	Fumio Yamaguchi and Hiromitsu Mori
Editor:	Reiko Kaneko

Assistant Director: Kenjiro Oomori
Stills: Naomi Hashiyama
Cast: Zushi Yoshitaka (Rokuchan), Kin Sugai (Okuni-san, Rokuchan's Mother), Kazuo Kato (Painter on the Roadside), Junzaburo Ban (Yukcihi Shima), Kiyoko Tange (Wife), Michio Hino (Ikawa, Friend of Mr. Shima), Tatsuhei Shimokawa (Nomoto, Friend of Mr. Shima), Keiji Furuyama (Matsui, Friend of Mr. Shima), Hisashi Igawa (Masuo Masuda, Casual Laborers), Hideko Okiyama (Tatsu, Mrs. Masuda), Kunie Tanaka (Hatsutaro or Hatsuan Kawaguchi, Casual Laborers), Jitsuko Yoshimura (Yoshie, Mrs. Kawaguchi) Koji Mitsui (Master of the Tavern), Shinsuke Miname (Ryotaro Sawagami), Yuko Kusunoki (Misao, Mrs. Sawagami), Toshiyuki Tonomura (Taro), Satoshi Hasegawa (Jiro), Kumiko Ono (Hanako), Tatsuhiko Yanashisa (Shiro), Mika Oshida (Umeko), Tatsuo Matsumura (Kyota Watanaka, Katsuko'S Uncle), Mari Tsuji (Otane, Katsuko's Aunt), Tomoko Yamazaki (Kastuko), Masahiko Kametani (Okabe, Young Employee at the Saké Store Isesho), Minoru Takashima (Policeman), Keiji Sakakida (Master of the Saké Shop), Noboru Mitani (Father), Hiroyuki Kawase (Son), Hiroshi Kiyama (Sushi Shop Proprietor), Michiko Araki (Madam of a Small Japanese Restaurant), Shoichi Kuwayama (Master of a Western-style Restaurant), Toki Shiozawa (Waitress), Hiroshi Akutagawa (Mr. Hei), Tomoko Naraoka (Woman, Ocho), Atsushi Watanabe (Mr. Tanba or Tamba), Kamatari Fujiwara (Old Man), Masahiko Tanimura (Mr. So, Small Greengrocers Store), Fujio Jely (Kumanbachi-no-Kichi), Kayako Sono (Wife), Kiyotaka Ishii, Mihoko Kaizuka (Children A and B), Hideaki Ezumi (Detective), Sanji Kojima (Thief), Akemi Negishi (Good-looking Housewife), Reiko Niimura, Yoshiko Maki, Toshiko Sakurai, Matsue Ono, Toriko Takahara (Housewives A, B, C, D, and E), Akira Hitoma, Kanji Ebata, Masahiko Ichimura, Masaya Nihei, Shin Ibuki (Men Calling Out to Misao A, B, C, D, and E)
Distribution: Toho
Running Time: 140 Minutes
Color: Eastmancolor
Released: October, 1970
U.S. Release: October 5, 1971

Synopsis

Tokyo. 1970. In a wasteland outside the city Rokuchan, a 14-year-old retarded boy, lives with his mother. Their house is filled with brightly colored drawings of trolly cars. Rokuchan spends his day driving an imaginary trolly, making the appropriate sounds, "Do Des Ka Den."

In the neighborhood live the following people: Mr. Tanba, a kindly old gentleman; Masuda and his wife Tatsu and their neighbors Hatsutaro and

Yoshie (both men are laborers and both drink to excess); Mr. Shima, a smallish man with a limp who believes the world is wonderful, and Mrs. Shima, his domineering wife; Ryo, the hairbrush maker, his wife Misao and their five children; Kyota, a stern man who lives off his wife and his niece, Katsuko, who makes paper flowers; Okabe, a young errand boy who loves Katsuko; Hei, a broken man who lives in a shack off by himself; Hornet Kichi, a married man; and an impoverished father and his six-year old son who must beg to stay alive.

During the day the women gather at the common faucet and gossip. Matsuda has an argument with Tatsu and finds solace in the arms of Yoshie. Hungry, the son visits the food shops in town. He brings back raw fish from a sushi shop. At home, tired, he crawls in bed next to his father. Together they design an imaginary home, which is visualized on the screen.

At 2 a.m., Katsuko still works at her flowers. In Tanba's house a thief intrudes, but flees when Tanba offers him money and begs him not to steal his tool box.

Next day Okabe gives Katsuko a candy bar and tells her she is working too hard. Outside Hei's shack a fortyish woman appears. When Hei returns she enters the house and helps him with his work, although no words pass between the two.

At the faucet, the women disapprovingly discuss the marital swap between Yoshi and Otatsu. Hornet Kichi chases his wife and children around with a sword until Tanba intervenes. At home Ryo stares at his children, trying to determine which are not his.

A friend, discouraged with life, comes to visit Tanba. Tanba sends him away with renewed hope. That evening Kyota, aroused by the sleeping Katsuko, rapes her. The son eats raw fish, despite a warning to cook it first. In his own house Ryo reassures his children that he loves them as a father.

Kyota's wife, Otane, returns home from the hospital. The police bring a thief to Tanba's house, but Tanba denies the entire incident. Mr. Shima brings home three guests. Although his wife is rude and insolent, Shima defends her good qualities.

At Hei's shack the woman begs forgiveness for running away with another man, but Hei is not able to forgive his wife. Katsuko discovers she is pregnant, but will not name the father. The little son is gravely ill with chronic diarrhea.

The police inform Kyota that Katsuko has seriously stabbed Okabe. Hei's wife leaves the shack, now glassy-eyed like her husband. Katsuko finally reveals the truth to the police and Okabe recovers. The son dies. Tanba helps the father bury the child.

At the faucet all the women are cheery. Rokuchan appears with his imaginary trolly and finally returns home for dinner.

26 DERSU UZALA, 1975

Producer:	Mosfilm and Toho
Director:	Akira Kurosawa
Photography:	Asakadru Nakai, Yuri Gantman, and Fiodor Dobronavov
Art Direction:	Y. Rakoha

Scenario: Akira Kurosawa and Yuri Nagibin, Based on a book *Dersu, the Hunter* by Vladimir Arseniev
Music: Isaac Shvarts
Cast: Maxim Munzuk (Dersu Uzala), Juri Solomine (Vladimir Arseniev), S. Danilchenko (Arseniev's Wife), Dima Kortishev (Vova, Arseniev's Son)
Distribution: Sovexport
Running Time: 137 Minutes
Format: 70 mm
Color: Color
Sound: Six-track Stereophonic
Released: August 12, 1975
U.S. Release: October 5, 1976

Synopsis

1910. Korfovskaia, Siberia. An army captain arrives seeking the grave of a man buried several years before, but already the trees have been cut down to make room for the growing village.

1902. A group of Russian soldiers on a topographical expedition move through the forest singing. The narrator, Capt. Vladimir Arseniev, tells of their chance meeting with Dersu Uzala, an old Mongolian hunter. Having lost all his family in a smallpox epidemic, he now lives alone in the wilds. Dersu agrees to become their guide. He teaches the men how to survive in the wilderness, and tries to impart to them his own respect for all living things. Dersu's wisdom and simple kindness greatly move Arseniev. In Dersu's uneducated mind all the elements of nature have a living spirit.

First the group comes upon a deserted hut and then an old Chinaman who has lived alone for forty years. Continually they move further north. Dersu and Arseniev push ahead traversing a lake in a dug-out and crossing marshes where no trails exist. In the frozen wasteland the silence is menacing.

Unexpectedly a strong wind gathers force. Dersu and Arseniev work frantically to cut dry grass and cover themselves in a makeshift hut. Dersu's knowledge saves their lives. Finally the two are reunited with the rest. The mission becomes harder as hunger and exhaustion set in. Crossing the tundra they find a family who provide them with hot food. The captain invites Dersu to return to the city with him, but Dersu declines the invitation.

1907. Spring. Again Arseniev and his men survey Siberia. Happily they again find Dersu. Moving through the forest they discover animal traps left by the Chinese. Compassionately they set the animals free. Next they come upon a ransacked village where the Chinese bandits have taken the women and left the men to die. Continuing down the river they unexpectedly hit rapids. During this endeavor Arseniev and his men save Dersu from drowning. A happy autumn follows during which time the captain photographs Dersu.

In the woods Dersu shoots at a tiger who has been following the group. Increasingly he grows moody, believing he has offended a forest god. When Dersu and Arseniev are out shooting, Dersu unexplainedly misses a deer and later a wild boor. Subsequently he is unable to hit a practice target. Gradually Dersu realizes his eyesight is failing. Again Arseniev offers Dersu a place in his home. Haunted by tiger spirits and unable to live in the forest with failing eyesight, Dersu accepts.

In Khaborovsk, Dersu lives with Arseniev and his family, but has difficulty adjusting to civilized life. Although he is well-treated by the captain's wife and admired by his son Vova, Dersu feels confined and unhappy. Humbly begging forgiveness he decides to return to the forest. As a parting present Arseniev gives him a new rifle with special sights.

Shortly after Dersu's departure Arseniev receives a telegram from the police. Arriving at the station, he discovers Dersu's corpse. Evidence indicates that Dersu was killed by a thief who desired the gun. The body is buried and Arseniev thrusts Dersu's walking stick into the top of the fresh mound.

Writings about Akira Kurosawa, 1951-1977

1951

27 Crowther, Bosley. "Intriguing Japanese Picture, *Rashomon*, First Feature at Rebuilt Little Carnegie." *The New York Times* (27 December), p. 18. Reprinted in *Focus on Rashomon*, 1972.
    Notes "brilliance" of the camera and calls "artful and fascinating."

28 McCarten, John. "What Happened in Those Woods?" *The New Yorker*, 27, no. 46 (29 December), 60. Reprinted in *Focus on Rashomon*, 1972.
    Adverse review. Calls film "simple-minded."

*29 Shimizu, Chiyota. "Throwing a Curved Ball into Love and Truth." *Kinema Jumpo* (April).
    An interview with Kurosawa cited in Jorgens (455).

30 Zunser, Jesse. "*Rashomon*." *Cue* (29 December), Reprinted in *Focus on Rashomon*, 1972).
    Calls film an "extraordinary motion picture" and an absorbing drama." Cites the "memorable visual setting."

1952

31 Anon. "New Films." *Newsweek*, 39, no. 1 (7 January), 59-60.
    Praises *Rashomon* as "a stunning work of art." Plot outline.

32 Anon. "The New Pictures." *Time*, 59, no. 1 (7 January), 82-84. Reprinted in *Focus on Rashomon*, 1972.
    Favorable review and background information on *Rashomon*. Plot synopsis and analysis.

33 Anon. "Japan's Great Film." *Life*, 32, no. 3 (21 January), 53-54.
    Favorable review. Plot outline.

34 Anon. "*Rashomon*." *Time*, 59, no. 1 (7 January), 82-83.
    Calls film "novel," but "flawed." Criticizes it as "draggy" and "self-conscious."

35 Barbarow, George. "*Rashomon* and the Fifth Witness." *Hudson Review*, 5, no. 3 (Autumn), 420-422. Reprinted in *Focus on Rashomon*, 1972.
   Unsympathetic review which criticizes film for its confusing presentation. However, praises the photographic artistry and visual beauty. Counters acceptance of film as a masterpiece and questions the reliance of the work on verbal information.

*36 Beaufort, John. *The Christian Science Monitor* (2 January). Reprinted in *Focus on Rashomon*, 1972.
   Review of *Rashomon*.

37 Crowther, Bosley. "*Rashomon*." *The New York Times* (6 January), p. II, 1. Reprinted in *Focus on Rashomon*, 1972.
   Cites work as the best foreign language film of the year. States it differs from other movies because it probes one episode rather than following a linear story-line.

38 Dent, Alan. "Mainly Non-Adult." *The Illustrated London News*, 220 (5 April), 592.
   Finds film almost too adult and too bizarre.

39 Falk, Ray. "Introducing Japan's Top Director." *The New York Times* (6 January), x-5.
   Criticism by Kurosawa of young Japanese directors who lack courage to tackle large projects. Includes directors' comments on contemporary films and some biographical data.

40 Farber, Manny. "*Rashomon*." *The Nation*, 174, no. 3 (19 January), 66. Reprinted in *Focus on Rashomon*, 1972.
   Brief review. Calls film "torpid," "stylish," and "Louvre-conscious."

41 Griffith, Richard. "An Almost Forgotten Art." *The Saturday Review*, 35, no. 3 (19 January), 33. Reprinted in *Focus on Rashomon*, 1972.
   Praises *Rashomon* as a "great film" and calls it one of the few grown-up movies. Claims it is a reminder of the great tradition of silent acting.

42 Harcourt-Smith, Simon. "*Rashomon*." *Sight and Sound*, 22, no. 1 (July-September), 28-29.
   Calls film an "extraordinary picture." Points out the necessity of putting it in a national context and comments on its political significance in Japan. Cites film's relationship to the Kabuki tradition.

43 Harrington, Curtis. "*Rashomon* et le cinema japonais." *Cahiers du cinéma*, no. 12 (May), pp. 53-57. Reprinted in *Focus on Rashomon*, 1972.
   Talks about the unique qualities of Japanese film in relation to the cinematic techniques borrowed from the West. Suggests that *Rashomon* and other Kurosawa films are literary in that they deal with form as a succession of physically poetic images. Notes Kurosawa's efforts to elicit audience participation.

44 Hart, Henry. "*Rashomon*." *Films in Review*, 3, no. 1 (January), 34-37.
   Favorable review with plot summary. Calls work a "major emotional experience." Praises Kurosawa's human insight and the film's artistry.

45 Hartung, Philip T. "Getting to Know You." *The Commonweal*, 55, no. 14 (11 January), 350.
Review and plot outline of *Rashomon*.

46 Kass, Robert. "Film and TV." *The Catholic World*, 174, no. 1043 (February), pp. 385-386.
Favorable review of *Rashomon*. Calls it a "remarkable film."

47 Kauffman, Stanley. "Movies." *The New Republic*, 126 (14 January), 22. Reprinted in *A World on Film*, 1966.
Mixed review of *Rashomon*. Finds film incredibly slow and humorless, but an "absorbing picture" with elegance.

48 McDonald, Gerald D. "New Films From Books." *Library Journal*, 77, no. 2 (15 January), 140.
Praises all aspects of the film. Plot synopsis.

49 Shigeno, Tatsuhiko. "Kurosawa Akira" [Akira Kurosawa]. *Kinema Jumpo* (1st half of April), pp. 38-41.
Criticizes Kurosawa's works for the literary language of the characters, especially *Stray Dog*. Feels this limits a clear distinction of personalities. Reservations about all films, even *Rashomon*, but admits appeal for foreign viewers.

50 Tyler, Parker. "*Rashomon* as Modern Art." *Cinema 16*, pamphlet one. New York. Reprinted in *Three Faces of the Film*, 1967, *Rashomon*, 1969. *Renaissance of the Film*, 1970, and *Focus on Rashomon*, 1972.
Calls film a Japanese masterpiece. Purpose of film not to decipher the truth. Film manifests multiplicity like modern painting. Original event (rape and murder) so horrifying that it creates own ambiguity. Sees confession as sin. Refers to *Rashomon* as a time mural.

51 Whitebait, William. "The Movies." *The New Statesman*, 43 (15 March), 302.
Favorable review of *Rashomon*. Compares impact of the movie to the power of an Eisenstein film. Plot summary.

1953

52 Anderson, Joseph L. "The History of Japanese Movies." *Films in Review*, 4 (June-July), 277-290.
Overview of Japanese film history with separate comments on Kurosawa, especially on *Rashomon* and *Ikiru*.

53 Mercier, Pierre. "*Rashomon* et le pédantisme." *Cahiers du cinéma*, no. 24 (June), pp. 38-40. Reprinted in *Focus on Rashomon*, 1972.
Brief discussion of the psychological ambiguities of the characters and the structure of the film. Also treats the rhythm of the scenes, counterpoint of sounds and images, spatial distribution of the actors within the frame, and symbolic images.

54   Sadoul, Georges. "Existe-t-il un néorealism japonais?" *Cahiers du cinéma,* no. 28 (November), pp. 7-19.
    Discusses Japanese neorealism in films between 1950 and 1953. Sees them on a par with earlier Italian works. Treats *Rashomon* within this context.

1954

55   Davidson, James F. "Memory of Defeat in Japan: A Reappraisal of *Rashomon.*" *The Antioch Review,* 14, no. 4 (December), 492-501. Reprinted in *Rashomon,* 1969, and *Focus on Rashomon,* 1972.
    Points out implications of *Rashomon* in terms of Japan's defeat and occupation. Stresses the importance of a setting of decay. Notes characterization of the thief as an oni (foreigner). Points out the need for hope at the end.

56   Leyda, Jay. "The Films of Kurosawa." *Sight and Sound,* 24, no. 2 (October-December), 74-78, 112. Reprinted in *The Thousand Eyes Magazine,* 1976.
    General praise of Kurosawa. Biographical information and plot summaries. Critical comments on works from *Sanshiro Sugata* to *Seven Samurai.* Discussion of Japanese preference for *Drunken Angel.* Reference to the "range," "humanity," "physical beauty," and "moral strength" found in Kurosawa's films, as well as the targets of his anger and disgust.

57   Rosenthal, A. "Humanism in Film." *Film,* no. 28 (October), pp. 38-40.
    Discusses the portrayal of relationships in Kurosawa's films and man's continual search for a better understanding of the self.

1955

58   Anon. "Le cinema japonais." *Cinema '55* [Paris], no. 6, (June-July), pp. 15-24.
    Discussion of social nature of Kurosawa's work. Notes the exception of *Rashomon.* Treats Kurosawa's desire to deal with ancient drama in a new way, as action film which portrays human nature. Contains a filmography from 1943 to 1954.

*59   Barnes, Peter. "*The Seven Samurai.*" *Films and Filming,* 1, no. 7 (April), 23.
    Review. Cited in Bowles, Stephen E. *Index to Critical Film Reviews,* vol. 2, New York: Burt Franklin & Co., 1975, p. 451.

60   Richard, Tony. "*Seven Samurai.*" *Sight and Sound,* 24, no. 4 (Spring), 195-196.
    Favorable review with some reservations. Compares Kurosawa with John Ford.

61   Rieupeyrout, Jean-Louis. "*Rashomon.*" *Cinéma '55* [Paris], no. 6 (June-July).
    Brief study of the film in terms of its relationship to the Western. Touches on the Pirandellian theme.

62   Strauss, Harold. "My Affair with Japanese Movies." *Harper's Magazine,* no. 1262 (July), 54-59.

Sets background for the surprise success of *Rashomon* in Venice, 1951, and its aftereffects. Also chronicles author's meeting with Kurosawa and their discussion on why Japanese films win prizes.

63 Young, Vernon. "The Japanese Film: Inquiries and Inferences." *The Hudson Review*, 8, no. 3 (Autumn), 836-842. Reprinted in *Focus on Rashomon*, 1972 and *On Film*, 1972.
Discusses the relationship between Japanese film and Japanese painting. Sees little connection. Challenges current use of the word "stylized." Deals with Kurosawa in the context of the whole Japanese cinema and stresses the need for exposure to more Japanese films.

64 _____. "Reflections on the Japanese Film." *Art Digest*, 29 (August), 20-21.
General article about Japanese film with special mention of *Rashomon*. Notes how Western audiences are seduced by style of Japanese films.

1956

*65 Anon. *Initiation au cinéma japonais.* Paris: Cinémathèque francaise.
Cited in Richie (269), p. 212.

66 Anon. "Japan-Style Western." *Newsweek*, 48, no. 24 (10 December), 119.
Favorable review of *Seven Samurai*. Plot outline.

67 Anon. "The New Pictures." *Time*, 68, no. 24 (10 December), 102-106.
Calls *Seven Samurai* an epic, but finds "something tiresome in all this sensuality." Feels film lacks a true sense of the "moral hell" of war.

68 Anon. "*The Seven Samurai.*" *The New York Times Magazine* (28 October), pp. 70-71.
Photographs from the film.

69 Crowther, Bosley. "*The Magnificent Seven.*" *The New York Times*, (20 November), p. 46.
Favorable review on every level. Calls the work "extraordinary."

70 Giuglaris, Shinobu and Marcel Giuglaris. *Le cinéma japonais, (1896-1955).* Paris: Editions du cerf, 245 pp. passim.
General history of the Japanese cinema. Treats film revolution caused by *Rashomon* in the making of historical films and the diversification which followed in its wake. Documents foreign success and reception in Japan. Quotes Kurosawa's belief that a film, whether traditional or modern, is above all the account of a psychological drama.

71 Hartung, Philip T. "Ode to the Warrior." *The Commonweal*, 65, no. 11 (14 December), 289-290.
Favorable review of *Seven Samurai*. Plot synopsis.

72 Hatch, Robert. "*The Seven Samurai.*" *The Nation*, 183, no. 23 (8 December), 507.
   Favorable review, especially for film's characterizations and photography.

73 Hines, T.S. "*The Seven Samurai.*" *Films in Review*, 7, no. 10 (December), 526.
   Adverse review. Feels film should be re-edited for U.S. art houses.

74 Knight, Arthur. "The Japanese Do It Again." *The Saturday Review*, 39, no. 48 (1 December), 54.
   Praises all aspects *Seven Samurai* and especially Kurosawa's ability to enliven and portray the past through his stories and characters. Plot synopsis.

*75 Leonard, Harold. "*Ikiru.*" U.C.L.A. Film Series Notes (25 March).
   Cited in Richie (269), p. 214.

76 Leyda, Jay. "Modesty and Pretension in Two New Films." *Film Culture*, 2, no. 4 (issue 10), 3-7, 27.
   Decries unimaginative flood of post-war "sword films." Remarks on the courage of Kurosawa's *Rashomon* and discusses its effect on the Japanese film industry. Comments on the greatness of *Seven Samurai*, especially its "artless art" and the manifestation of Zen Buddhist philosophy within the work.

77 McCarten, John. "East is West." *The New Yorker*, 32, no. 41 (1 December), 129.
   Mixed reactions to *Seven Samurai*. Praises characterization, but finds the acting "excessively emotional."

*78 Mills, William E. "*Rashomon.*" *Film Journal* [Melbourne], no. 6 (December), p. 6-9.
   Cited in Bowles, Stephen E. *Index to Critical Film Reviews*, vol. 2, New York: Burt Franklin & Co., 1975, p. 413.

*79 _____. "*The Seven Samurai.*" *Film Journal* [Melbourne], pp. 6-9.
   Cited in Bowles, Stephen E. *Index to Critical Film Reviews*, vol. 2, New York: Burt Franklin & Co., 1975, p. 451.

80 Miner, Earl Roy. "Japanese Film Art in Modern Dress.'" *Quarterly of Film, Radio, and Television*, 10, no. 4 (Summer), 354-363.
   Review of six Japanese films shown in Los Angeles in mid-fifties, including *Doomed* [*Ikiru*]. Calls it "one of the greatest films of our time."

1957

81 Anon. "Personality of the Month." *Films and Filming*, 4, no. 2 (November), p. 5.
   Biographical information and photograph of Kurosawa.

82 Anon. "Wild West Out East: Fight and Fury Fill Japanese Film, *The Magnificent Seven.*" *Life*, 42, no. 2 (14 January), p. 92.
   Favorable review. Plot synopsis. Compares 16th century Japan to U.S. Wild West.

83   Anderson, Lindsay. "Two Inches Off the Ground." *Sight and Sound*, 27, no. 3 (Winter), 131-133, 160.
    Cites the benefit of the National Film Theatre series to see accomplishments of post-1930 Japanese cinema. Calls Kurosawa the most modern of the directors and praises his experimentation in the narrative structure in *Ikiru*. Gives plot summary.

84   B.[azin], A.[ndre]. "Vivre." *Cahiers du cinéma*, no. 69 (March), pp. 36-37.
    Opposes critical opinion of Moullet (#89). Finds *Living [Ikiru]* perhaps the most beautiful, most expert, most moving among all the modern Japanese films. Discusses Western influences on Kurosawa's work. Feels certain elitism in France has prejudiced audiences against Kurosawa.

85   Gaffary, F. "Les deux visages d'Akira Kurosawa." *Positif*, no. 22, pp. 2-10.
    Notes on the wartime productions with specific attention to *The Men Who Tread on the Tiger's Tail*. Critical comments, historical background on Kurosawa's studio changes, financial information, casts, and awards for films from 1947-1955. Comments on the influence of Zen Buddhism on the samurai films. Reference to *Seven Samurai* as the summit of Kurosawa's work, a successful synthesis of two tendencies: social humanity and unusual adventure.

86   Iwasaki, Akira and Akira Kurosawa. "Kunonosujo o Megutte Ohfuku Shokan" [About Kumonosu Castle]. *Eiga Hyoron* (March), pp. 46-51.
    Four letters, two by each man. Iwasaki praises *The Throne of Blood* as a progressive step in a new direction, especially in its use of Noh elements. Feels film more important than *Rashomon* as a successful experiment. Contrasts Kurosawa with Ozu and Naruse who reflect only a Japanese point of view. Reply by Kurosawa stresses love for beauty and serenity of Noh which communicates through the heart, not the head.

87   Knight, Arthur. *The Liveliest Art*. New York: Macmillan, pp. 230-231.
    Reflects the period when Kurosawa's works were still unavailable in the West. Discusses *Rashomon* as an allegory which questions the old truth of blind obedience to the emperor against the new truth of democratization.

88   *A Light in the Japanese Window*. London: British Film Institute, 16 pp.
    Critical comments on the fourteen features shown for the first series of Japanese films at the National Film Theatre. Includes films by Kurosawa.

*89 Moullet, Luc. "La rétrospective Kurosawa à la Cinémathèque." *Cahiers du cinéma*, no. 68 (February).
    Cited in Richie (269), p. 214.

90   Suda, Motoji. "Kurosawa's *Macbeth*." *Film Journal* [Melbourne], no. 8 (July), pp. 3-4.
    Sees film as a "stark drama," but feels "Shakespeare's romanticism and Japanese formalism mix oddly." Considers Kurosawa's work as an urge to delve into human mind and to achieve purity of form.

91   Thirard, Paul-Louis. "La lagune des regrets, Venise 57." *Positif*, nos. 25-26 (Summer), p. 35.
    Brief comment on *The Throne of Blood*. Feels the film deserves a Golden Lion. Praises it on all levels and calls the work "full of genius."

1958

92 Anderson, Joseph L. and Donald Richie. "Traditional Theater and the Film in Japan." *Film Quarterly*, 12, no. 1 (Fall), 2-9.
   Questions the influence of Kabuki and Noh on Japanese film. Sees little direct connection except a pervasive Japanese sensibility in all three art forms.

93 Cavander, Kenneth. "*Throne of Blood.*" *Sight and Sound*, 27, no. 5 (Summer), 250.
   Adverse review. Sees film as a poor adaptation lacking in personal vision, and sublety, character motivation and tension, and with nothing to replace Shakespeare's speeches.

94 Fox, Charles. "*Throne of Blood.*" *Film*, no. 15 (January-February), pp. 22-23.
   Mixed reaction to the film.

95 Kirby, Gordon. "Who's Who in the Japanese Cinema." *Film Journal* [Melbourne], no. 11 (October), pp. 22-28.
   Biographical and critical summation, followed by a filmography.

1959

96 Anon. "Akira Kurosawa: World Famed Film Director," in *Profiles*. Clipping files Museum of Modern Art, Film Study Center, pp. 43-59.
   Biographical data. Plot summaries and quotations from contemporary Japanese reviews for all films up to *The Hidden Fortress*. Very concise overview of Kurosawa's work.

97 Anderson, Joseph L. and Donald Richie. *The Japanese Film: Art and Industry.* Tokyo and Rutland, Vt.: Charles E. Tuttle, pp. 223-227, 272-275, 376-380, passim." Reprinted in paperback by Grove Press, 1960.
   References to Kurosawa's whole career throughout the work. Special attention to *Rashomon* and *Seven Samurai*. Career essay at end of book.

98 Crowther, Bosley. "*Drunken Angel.*" *The New York Times* (31 December), p. 12.
   Favorable review with some reservations concerning the film's "crude, derivative techniques."

99 Dyer, Peter John. "*Ikiru.*" *Films and Filming*, 5, no. 11 (August), 25.
   Favorable review with reservations about Shimura's calculated performance. Plot summary. Compares Kurosawa with de Sica.

100 Holmes, Winifred, ed. *Orient: A Survey of Films.* London: British Film Institute, 90 pp.
   A survey of films produced in Arab and Asian countries. The first part includes features by Kurosawa with plot synopses and credits.

101 Myro. "*Kakushitoride No Sanakunin (Three Rascals in a Hidden Fortress).*" *Variety*, (8 July), p. 6.

Favorable review. Calls the film one of the best examples of recent Japanese filmmaking — "high grade direction." Feels film "somewhat over-long, however."

102   Vance, James S. *"Donzoko"* [*The Lower Depths*]. *Film Quarterly*, 13, no. 2 (Winter), p. 52.
Brief review. Calls work a "brave enterprise."

103   No entry.

1960

104   Anon. *"Drunken Angel." Filmfacts*, 3, p. 5.
Plot synopsis, credits, and excerpts from American reviewers.

105   Anon. *"Ikiru." Filmfacts*, 3, p. 37.
Plot synopsis, credits, and excerpts from American reviewers.

106   Anon. *"Ikiru." Time*, 75, no. 7 (15 February), 85.
Sees heroic defects, but calls film a "masterwork of burning social conscience and hard-eyed psychological realism."

107   Anon. *"The Men Who Tread on a Tiger's Tail." Filmfacts*, 3, p. 16.
Plot synopsis, credits, and excerpts from American reviewers.

108   Anby. *"Drunken Angel." Variety* (3 February).
Favorable review. Calls the film "most effective" and refers to its "searching views of contemporary Japanese life." Feels the work deserves serious consideration.

109   Anby. *"The Men Who Tread on the Tiger's Tail." Variety*, (27 January), p. 6.
Favorable review. Claims picture needs notes, but feels discriminating audiences "should find much of interest."

110   Anderson, Joseph L. and Donald Richie. *The Japanese Film: Art and Industry*. New York: Grove Press, 456 pp. First published by Charles E. Tuttle, 1959, 456 pp. Reprint of entry no. 97.

111   Bernhardt, William. *"Ikiru." Film Quarterly*, 13, no. 4 (Summer), 39-41.
Favorable review. Gives background on Kurosawa's work, a plot synopsis, and film analysis, especially of movie's narrative structure.

112   Crowther, Bosley. *"Ikiru." The New York Times* (30 January), p. 13.
Favorable review with reservations concerning the last 45 minutes of flashbacks.

113   H., J. *"The Hidden Fortress." Film Quarterly*, 13, no. 3 (Spring), p. 59.
Brief note. Calls film "a John Ford Western."

114   Kauffmann, Stanley. "The Fact of Mortality." *The New Republic*, 142, no. 10 (7 March), 28. Reprinted in *A World on Film*, 1966.

Compares *Ikiru* to Tolstoy's *Ivan Ilych*. Says "hard to overpraise Akira Kurosawa's direction," but does find funeral scene "too fully explored." Notes universality of the work. Plot synopsis.

115 Knight, Arthur. "Season in the Sun." *The Saturday Review*, 43, no. 7 (13 February), 40.
Comments on *Rashomon, The Men Who Tread on the Tiger's Tail*, and *Ikiru*. Compares Kurosawa with Ingmar Bergman. Sees both directors as symbols of the individualist — the complete filmmaker.

116 McCarten, John. "Unexpected Blend." *The New Yorker*, 35, no. 48 (16 January), 94.
Favorable review of *The Men Who Tread on the Tiger's Tail* detailing the film's suppression in Japan. Plot synopsis.

117 Mekas, Jonas. "Drunken Angel." *The Village Voice* (13 January), p. 8. Reprinted in *Movie Journal*, 1972.
Calls work "a dark, moody poem" and "a desperate stone that Kurosawa swings into the very face of man."

118 _____. "Movie Journal." *The Village Voice* (10 February), p. 8, 10.
Favorable review of *Ikiru*. Criticizes American critics who don't understand the horizontal construction of Kurosawa's work.

119 Richie, Donald. "Akira Kurosawa," in *Who's Who in Japan*. Tokyo: The Rengo Press.
Deals with Kurosawa's contribution as a filmmaker. Contains biographical details.

120 _____. "A Personal Record." *Film Quarterly*, 14, no. 1 (Fall), 20-30.
Conversations and memories of important people in post-war Japanese film industry. Includes Kurosawa.

121 Roemer, Michael. "Kurosawa's Way of Seeing." *Reporter*, 22, no. 6 (17 March), 36-38.
Recognition of Kurosawa as an artist of first rank despite release of only five films in U.S. to date. Sees Kurosawa's work as fresh approach to filmmaking. Sees camera work as the key to his style. Special comments on master works *Ikiru* and *The Magnificent Seven*.

122 Roman, Robert C. "*Ikiru*." *Films in Review*, 11, no. 3 (March), 168.
Review with plot summary.

123 Thompson, Howard. "The Men Who Tread on the Tiger's Tail." *The New York Times* (11 January), p. 35.
Reserved review. Calls the film an "oddity," not for those without some knowledge of Kabuki drama.

124 Tozzi, Romano. "Drunken Angel." *Films in Review*, 11, no. 2, (February), 105.
Mixed reaction. Calls film "uneven."

1961

125 Anon. "Kurosawa's *Macbeth*." *Time*, 78, no. 22 (1 December), 76.
Calls the film the "most brilliant and original attempt ever made to put Shakespeare in pictures."

126 Anon. "Lay On, Kunimaru." *Newsweek*, 58, no. 22 (27 November), 88-89.
Brief review of *The Throne of Blood*. Emphasis on Kurosawa's use of sound.

127 Clarens, Carlos. "Throne of Blood." *Films in Review*, 12, no. 10 December), 622.
Mixed reactions. Finds film "gorgeously exotic," but "coldly perfect and passionless."

128 Crowther, Bosley. "Throne of Blood." *The New York Times* (23 November), p. 50.
Adverse review. Treats the film as a serio-comic rendering and calls it a "grotesquely brutish and barbaric horse-opera."

129 Foster, Hugh G. "Japan: The Peculiar Films." *Holiday*, 30, no. 4 (October), 112-113, 116.
Based on viewing twelve Japanese films which Foster found lacking in humor and plot progression. Calls *Ikiru* sentimental — "unrelieved dolor." Equates it with the feel of Hollywood studio films.

130 Gill, Brendan. "Evil Thoughts." *The New Yorker*, 37, no. 42 (2 December), 126-127.
Favorable review of *The Throne of Blood*. Special mention of costumes.

131 Gow, Gordon. "The Hidden Fortress." *Films and Filming*, 7, no. 8 May, 27.
Mixed reactions. Feels the film has its moments. Especially likes Kurosawa's flair for composition, cutting and uninhibited action. Reservations about the acting.

132 Hartung, Philip T. "Tomorrow and Tomorrow." *The Commonweal*, 75, no. 11 (8 December), pp. 284-285.
Favorable review of *The Throne of Blood*. Compares it with Shakespeare's *Macbeth*.

133 Hawk. "Yojimbo," ("The Bodyguard"). *Variety* (30 August), p. 6.
Favorable review. Calls film "rousing, good story, told with vigor and visual excitement." Plot summary.

134 Iwabutchi, M[asayoshi]. "Japanese Cinema 1961." *Film Culture*, no. 24 (Spring), pp. 85-88.
Treats the effect of TV on Japanese film production and the major shifts within the industry. Discusses the success of *Yojimbo* and *Sanjuro* at the box office in Japan and Kurosawa's interest in the Western. Brief plot summaries.

135 Kauffmann, Stanley. "*Macbeth* in Japan, Stale Smoke in Dixie." *The New Republic*, 145, no. 22 (27 November), 18.

Finds the film inaccessible. Points up the gap in cultural understanding. Calls the film "an exotically distorting mirror."

*136 Leirens, Jean. "Akira Kurosawa." *Amis du Film*, no. 69 (September).
Cited in Richie (269), p. 214.

137 MacDonald, Dwight. "Films." *Esquire*, 61, no. 2 (August), 116. Reprinted in *On Movies*, 1969.

Review of *The Hidden Fortress*. Feels the film reveals Kurosawa's two weaknesses: "a tendency to over-labor and repeat ... and the mingling of incompatible genres." Calls the film a "potboiler."

138 _____. "Throne of Blood." *Esquire*, 57, (March), 22. Reprinted in *On Movies*, 1969.

Finds the film a "cops and robbers" movie with marvelous photography. Calls it a melodrama which "becomes monotonous."

139 McVay, Douglas. "The Rebel in a Kimono." *Films and Filming*, 7, no. 10 (July), 9-10, 34.

Places Kurosawa in context with other Japanese directors. Detailed description of *Rashomon* and *Ikiru*.

140 _____. "Samurai and Small Beer." *Films and Filming*, 7, no. 11 (August), 15-16.

Detailed description of *Seven Samurai, The Throne of Blood, The Lower Depths* and *The Hidden Fortress*.

141 Quigly, Isabel. "The Hidden Fortress." *The Spectator*, no. 6925, (17 March), p. 368.

Mixed reactions. Claims the film has "many of the ingredients of success, but somehow not mixed successfully."

142 Richie, Donald. *Japanese Movies*. Tokyo: Japan Travel Bureau, 198 pp. Reprinted as *Japanese Cinema: Film Style and National Character* by Doubleday, 1971.

Long section on Kurosawa as master stylist, who combines aesthetics and social issues in one work. Sees strong character motivation and an environmental context for every action. Calls Kurosawa's work a departure from traditional Japanese cinema and deals with question of Western/Eastern sensibilities. Refers to Kurosawa's interest in Dostoyevsky, his humanism and moral outlook. Specific references to individual films.

143 _____. *Kurosawa Retrospektive XI*. Internationale Filmfestspiele. Berlin. 17 pp.

A program booklet mostly in German. Contains an introductory essay in English, an essay "A Note on Kurosawa's Style," and a filmography from 1943 to 1961.

144 Torok, Jean-Paul. "Venise 61." *Positif*, no. 43, pp. 12-13.

Discusses *Yojimbo*, stating that the naïveté of the image conceals the complexity of the motif too well. However, praises the film and claims that Kurosawa is "a notch above Ichikawa — the best Japanese filmmaker."

145 Young, Vernon. "*The Hidden Fortress*: Kurosawa's Comic Mode." *The Hudson Review*, 16, no. 2 (Summer), 270-275. Reprinted in *On Film*, 1972.

Treats dynamism and physicality of Kurosawa's work, especially *The Hidden Fortress*. Deals with his use of the wide screen. Includes comments on *Seven Samurai* and *Ikiru*. Talks of Kurosawa's treatment of men as animal-like and reveals how he characterizes them through types.

1962

146 Anon. "Bad Guys vs. Bad Guys." *Newsweek*, 60, no. 17 (22 October), 104.

Review of *Yojimbo*. Treats the film as both a Western and a gangster picture using Robert Warshow's definition.

147 Anon. "*The Hidden Fortress*." *Filmfacts*, 5, p. 31.

Plot synopsis, credits, and excerpts from American reviewers.

148 Anon. "Japanese Apocalypse." *Time*, 80 (21 September), 90.

Favorable review of *Yojimbo*. Calls film a "master-piece of misanthropy" and calls Kurosawa "a cracking satirist" on the level of Bertolt Brecht. Gives biographical information on Kurosawa and comments on his major films and themes.

149 Anon. "Oh, The Way People Live!" *Time*, 79, no. 10 (9 March), 91.

Review of *The Lower Depths*. Calls the film a "fascinating minor work by a continually amazing major artist."

150 Anon. "*Yojimbo*." *Filmfacts*, 5, p. 275.

Plot synopsis, credits, and excerpts from American reviewers.

151 Alpert, Hollis. "A Wandering Samurai." *The Saturday Review*, 45, no. 37 (15 September), 26.

Favorable review of *Yojimbo*, especially for Mifune and the scenario. Notes influence of *Shane* and *High Noon*.

152 Anderson, Joseph L. "When the Twain Meet: Hollywood's Remake of *Seven Samurai*." *Film Quarterly*, 15, no. 13 (Spring), 55-58.

Discusses similarities and differences between Kurosawa's *Seven Samurai* and the Hollywood remake, *The Magnificent Seven*. Refers to Kurosawa's allowance for ambiguity, his sparing use of the wide-angle lens and his restraint of dialogue. Concludes Kurosawa is a true *auteur*.

*153 Bernhardt, William. "*The Throne of Blood*." *For Film* (Winter).

Cited in Richie (269), p. 213.

154 Crowther, Bosley. "*The Hidden Fortress*." *The New York Times* (24 January), p. 24.

Plot summary. Calls the film a "pot-boiler," though entertaining and essentially "superficial."

155 ———. "The Lower Depths." *The New York Times* (10 February), p. 12.
Favorable review. Claims "Kurosawa's dark imagistic technique achieves its depressing aim."

156 ———. "Yojimbo." *The New York Times* (16 October), p. 34.
Plot summary. Mixed reactions.

157 Dillingham, Harold. "Yojimbo." *Films in Review*, 13, no. 9 (November) 561.
Adverse review. Calls film "not too interesting."

158 Gill, Brendan. "Man's Fate." *The New Yorker*, 37 (17 February), 117-119.
Favorable review of *The Lower Depths*. Calls the film "near perfect" and claims it cannot be overpraised. Treats film's universality and manner of production.

159 Hartung, Philip T. "The Mores the Merrier." *The Commonweal*, 77, no. 3 (12 October), 72-73.
Favorable review of *Yojimbo*, especially for Mifune's performance. Plot synopsis.

*160 Hull, David Stewart. "The Bad Sleep Well." *The U.C.L.A. Film Series Notes* (Fall).
Cited in Richie (269), p. 214.

161 Kauffmann, Stanley. "Masters New and Old." *The New Republic*, 146, no. 12 (19 March), 28. Reprinted in *A World On Film*, 1966.
Reviews of *The Lower Depths* and *The Hidden Fortress*. Calls the former "substantial but clumsy on the screen," and the latter "cinematically fine, but thin in content."

162 ———. "An Unemployed Samurai." *The New Republic*, 147, no. 12 (17 September), 27-28. Reprinted in *A World on Film*, 1966.
Favorable review of *Yojimbo*, especially for Kurosawa's "technical mastery," "freshness of vision" and "dramatic instinct." Compares the film with *Shane* and *The Gunfighter*. Likens Mifune to Spencer Tracy.

163 MacDonald, Dwight. "Films." *Esquire*, 58, no. 6 (December), 26, 34. Reprinted in *On Movies*, 1969.
Reserved review of Kurosawa's "latest Eastern Western," *Yojimbo*. Feels the film is a poor mimicry of the West and lacks a normative character.

164 Mekas, Jonas. "The Movie Journal." *The Village Voice* (8 February), p. 11.
Favorable review of *The Lower Depths*. Calls the film one of Kurosawa's better efforts. Compares it with two dramas: *The Connection* and *Waiting for Godot*. Agrees with Jay Leyda that Kurosawa's contemporary works may be superior to his period pieces.

165 ———. "Movie Journal." *The Village Voice* (25 October), p. 13.

Review of *Yojimbo*. Calls the film a "folk epic a la Brecht," "a morality movie." Likes the work but thinks it is "too simple."

166 Richie, Donald. "Akira Kurosawa." *Orient-West* [Tokyo], (Summer), pp. 45-55.
General comments on Kurosawa's style and themes, especially social issues in films like *Ikiru*. Biographical data. Description of the major films.

167 _____. "Dostoevsky with a Japanese Camera." *Horizon*, 4 (July), 42-47. Reprinted in *The Emergence of Film Art*, 1969.
Deals with Kurosawa's love and regard for Dostoyevsky and how his works have influenced Kurosawa's films. Comments on the Eastern and Western elements in these films.

168 S.B.I. "Kurosawa: Japan's Poet Laureate of Film." *Show Business Illustrated*, (April), pp. 28-29. Reprinted as "Akira Kurosawa" in *Film Makers on Film Making*, 1967.
General article about Kurosawa's life, training, and films.

169 Tube. *"Sanjuro." Variety* (30 June).
Favorable review. Refers to the "formidable hero" and predicts that the film will become a favorite with Japanese audiences.

170 Tyler, Parker. "Rashomon," in *Classics of the Foreign Film: A Pictorial Treasury*. New York: Citadel, pp. 192-195.
Plot summary. Discusses use of flashbacks. Background on the film. Well illustrated.

171 West, Anthony. "The Art of Akira Kurosawa." *Show*, 2, no. 7 (July), 58-62.
Explains why Kurosawa is considered the most Western Japanese director. Comments on his interest in people and making movies that say something. Specific references to *The Men Who Tread on the Tiger's Tail*, *Rashomon*, *The Throne of Blood*, *The Lower Depths* and modern dramas. Demonstrates Kurosawa's interest in the contemporary period even in historical films. Shows how he turns popular literary genres on their head.

172 Wharton, Flavia. *"The Lower Depths." Films in Review*, 13, no. 3 (March), 175-176.
Adverse review. Feels Kurosawa's attempts to translate Western classics into Japanese films succeeds "less and less."

1963

173 Anby. *"Ikimono No Kiroku" ("I Live in Fear"). Variety* (18 September), p. 6.
Luke-warm response. Feels theme "imperfectly articulated" by the characters although reviewer sees merit in the subject.

174 Anon. "Akira Kurosawa." Trans. by Yoshio Kamii. *Cinema* [Los

Angeles], 1, no. 5 (August-September), 27-28. Reprinted in *Kurosawa*, n.d., (**460**).
Discusses American directors, Westerns, use of actors, use of sound and camera movement.

*175   Anon. "The Bad Sleep Well." *Cinema* [Los Angeles], 1, no. 1, 29-31.
Cited in Batty, Linda. *Retrospective Index to Film Periodicals, 1930-1971*. New York: R.R. Bowker, 1975, p. 187.

176   Anon. "The Bad Sleep Well." *Filmfacts*, 6, p. 29.
Plot synopsis, credits, and excerpts from American reviewers.

177   Anon. "Gentleman of Japan." *Time*, 81, no. 4 (25 January), p. 42.
Plot summary of *The Bad Sleep Well*. States the film is not as strong as Kurosawa's strongest picture, but it has "vulgar energy."

178   Anon. "High and Low." *Filmfacts*, 6, p. 309.
Plot synopsis, credits, and excerpts from American reviewers.

179   Anon. "Japanese Sandman." *Newsweek*, 61, no. 5 (4 February), 78.
Adverse review of *The Bad Sleep Well*. Plot summary and analysis.

180   Anon. "Kurosawa." Trans. by Hideo Sekiguchi. *Cinema* [Los Angeles], 1, no. 5 (August-September), 28-31.
Emphasis on "the beauty of construction" of twenty-two Kurosawa films and the element of primitivism. Liberal quotations from Kurosawa.

181   Anon. "The Lone Samurai." *Newsweek*, 61, no. 20 (20 May), 103.
Adverse review of *Sanjuro*. States the "physical excesses" are no match for *Yojimbo*.

182   Anon. "The Lower Depths." *Cinema* [Los Angeles], 1, no. 2, p. 34.
Brief note. Refers to "visual magic" of the film.

183   Anon. "Mysterious East." *Newsweek*, 62, no. 22 (25 November), 105-106.
Favorable review of *High and Low*. Plot outline. Credits Kurosawa with establishing new trend in detective films.

*184   Anon. *A Retrospective of Japanese Cinema*. Tokyo: Japanese Cinémathèque, Tokyo Museum of Modern Art (in Japanese).
Cited in Richie (**269**), p. 212.

185   Anon. "Sanjuro." *Cinema* [Los Angeles], 1, no. 2, p. 30.

186   Anon. "Sanjuro." *Filmfacts*, 6, p. 134.
Plot synopsis, credits, and excerpts from American reviewers.

187   Anon. "Throne of Blood." *Cinema* [Los Angeles], 1, no. 1, p. 44.
Brief note. Refers to "visual art" and calls film "Kurosawa at his best!"

188 Anon. "Unkind Cut." *Newsweek*, 61, no. 18 (6 May), 94-95.
Documents Shochiku's editing of Kurosawa's four-and-a-half hour version of *The Idiot*. Gives plot outline.

189 Anon. "A Yen for Yen." *Time* 61 (29 November), pp. E3-E4.
Favorable review of *High and Low*. Calls the film "crackling with excitement" and "alive with motion." Plot summary.

190 Alpert, Hollis. "Fitful Slumber." *The Saturday Review*, 46, no. 3 (19 January), 24.
Disappointed review of *The Bad Sleep Well*. Objects to the melodramatic treatment.

191 Crist, Judith. "87th Precinct — Japanese Style." *The New York Herald Tribune* (8 December), p. 37. Reprinted in *The Private Eye, the Cowboy and the Very Naked Girl*, 1968.
Discusses the differences between Ed McBain's *King's Ransom* and Kurosawa's *High and Low*. Claims the "artist has taken over where the whodunit writer merely began." Shows how the accumulation of detail forms "a tapestry of crime, detection and punishment."

192 Crowther, Bosley. "*The Bad Sleep Well*." *The New York Times* (23 January), p. 5.
Favorable review. Calls the film "forceful" and "engrossing."

193 _____. "*Sanjuro*." *The New York Times* (8 May), p. 34.
Plot synosis. Mixed reactions.

194 Dillingham, Harold. "*The Bad Sleep Well*." *Films in Review*, 14, no. 2 (February), 113.
Adverse review, but high praise for Mifune. Calls the film "clumsy."

195 Gill, Brendan. "Good Out of Evil." *The New Yorker*, 39, no. 12 (11 May), 103.
Favorable review of *Sanjuro*. Plot synopsis.

196 _____. "Old Hands." *The New Yorker*, 39, no. 43 (14 December), 197-198.
Favorable review of *High and Low*. Plot synopsis.

197 Hartung, Philip T. "Can Spring Be Far Behind?" *The Commonweal*, 77, no. 20 (8 February), 517.
Disappointed review of *The Bad Sleep Well*. Outlines the film's faults.

198 _____. "How to Travel Without Moving." *The Commonweal*, 78, no. 7 (10 May), 198.
Mixed review of *The Idiot*. Praises techniques, photography and character development. Sees the experiments as old-fashioned.

199 Hashimoto, Shinobu. "Rashomon no Toji" [*Rashomon's* Own Time], in

Nihon Eiga Kaikoroku [*A Retrospective of Japanese Cinema*]. Tokyo: pp. 238-239.

Reveals the motivation for making *Rashomon* — desire to make first movie based on a story by Ryunosuke Akutagawa. Choice of "In a Grove" totally arbitrary.

200 Hawk. "Tengoku To — Jigoku" ("High and Low"). *Variety*, (4 September), p. 20.

Mixed review. Calls film "engrossing and neatly directed" but overlong. Brief plot summary.

201 Iida, Shinbi. "Kurosawa." Trans. by Hideo Sekiguchi. *Cinema* [Los Angeles], 1, no. 5 (August-September), 28-31. Reprinted in *Kurosawa*, n.d. (**465**).

Emphasizes "the beauty of construction" in twenty-two Kurosawa films. Deals with primitivism. Liberal quotations from the director.

202 Iijima, Tadashi, "Nihon Eiga Kaikoroku" [A Retrospective of Japanese Cinema], in *Nihon Eiga Kaikoroku* [*A Retrospective of Japanese Cinema*]. Tokyo: pp. 235-237.

Demonstrates how major characteristics of all twenty-three Kurosawa films are evident in his maiden work, *Sanshiro Sugata* — spiritualization, excellent cinematic technique, transition from tranquility to action, and a monomaniacal grasp of theme. Calls Kurosawa the most precious and unique Japanese director.

203 Kael, Pauline. "Body and Soul." *The Partisan Review*, 30 (Summer), 231-234. Reprinted in *I Lost It at the Movies*, 1965 and *Film Theory and Criticism*, 1974.

Discusses the "Eastern Western," *Yojimbo*, in which Kurosawa turns the conventions of the genre "inside out." According to Kael, he "liberates us from the pretensions of our 'serious Westerns.' "

204 Kauffmann, Stanley. "A Cold Season." *The New Republic*, 148, no. 19 (11 May), p. 27.

Adverse review of *The Idiot* which criticizes the film's length and lack of style and power.

205 _____. "From Bad to Worse." *The New Republic*, 148, no. 4 (26 January), 26. Reprinted in *A World on Film*, 1966.

Adverse review of *The Bad Sleep Well*. Calls it "remote in every way." Finds one reward, in Mifune's performance.

206 _____. "Japanese Drama, Domestic Japery." *The New Republic*, 149, no. 21 (23 November), 26-29. Reprinted in *A World on Film*, 1966.

Favorable review of *High and Low*. Questions why Kurosawa chose to make the film, but calls it "flawlessly executed" and "brilliantly right."

207 _____. "A Near Hit: More Art Than Matter." *The New Republic*, 148, no. 21 (25 May), 28.

Brief review of *Sanjuro*. Calls film "superb," but content "shallow."

208 Kurosawa, Akira. "Jokantoku Jidai no Omoide" [Recollections of My Time as an Assistant Director], in *Nihon Eiga Kaikoroku*, [*A Retrospective of Japanese Cinema*]. Tokyo, p. 237.
   Kurosawa recalls the words of Seami Kawatake, "Never forget your first decision." Claims this motto keeps him continually a fresh man in the movie industry.

209 _____. "Waga Eiga Jinsei no Ki" [Diary of My Movie Life]. *Kinema Jumpo*, Special Issue (April), pp. 50-65.
   Detailed biography of Kurosawa's early life, entry into the film industry, and comments on his films up through *High and Low*.

*210 Langlois, Henri and Tokawa Naoki. Preface, in *Chefs-d'oeuvre et panorama du cinéma japonais, 1898-1961, un hommage à la cinémathèque japonaise*. Paris: Cinémathèque francaise Paris, Exposition.
   Unverified.

211 Mekas, Jonas. "Movie Journal." *The Village Voice* (24 January), pp. 23, 25.
   Review of *The Bad Sleep Well*. Feels film is excellently played, but arty and self-conscious. Calls it "audio-visual vanity."

212 Myro. "*The Bad Sleep Well*." *Variety* (5 July), p. 7.
   Adverse review. States that "despite occasional flashes of directional brilliance" film is a disappointment. Says it should be re-edited.

213 Richie, Donald. "The Face of '63 — Japan." *Films and Filming*, 9, no. 10 (July), 9-10.
   Discusses economics and the industry's falling standards of excellence. Deals with the popularity of Kurosawa's *High and Low, Yojimbo*, and *Sanjuro*. However, feels these films are less artistically successful than *The Throne of Blood* and *The Lower Depths*.

214 _____. "Heaven and Hell." *Films and Filming*, 9, no. 4 (January), pp. 93-94.
   Report from location shooting. Description of Kurosawa's work methods. Also contains information on the making of *The Lower Depths*.

215 _____. "Kurosawa Hihyo o Hihyo Suru" [Kurosawa: A Foreign View of the Japanese View], *Kinema Jumpo*, no. 338 (25 March).
   An analysis of the critical response to Kurosawa in Japan and the West. Concludes that Western critics are more sensitive to Kurosawa's intent since they are undisturbed by the "Japaneseness" of his works.

216 _____. "The Ransom." *Film Quarterly*, 17, no. 2 (Winter), 47-48.
   Disappointed review of *High and Low*. Deals with the film as a two-part work: statement and conclusion. Compares with *Stray Dog* and calls *High and Low* "minor Kurosawa."

217 Shirai, Yoshio. "John Ford to Kurosawa Akira" [John Ford and Akira Kurosawa]. *Kinema Jumpo*, Special Issue, Kurosawa Akira: Sono Sakuhin to Kao [Akira Kurosawa: His Films and Face] (April), pp. 84-85.

Documents the meeting between Kurosawa and Ford in 1957 at the London Film Festival. Reveals the father-son relationship between the two and a common thread of dynamic and manly expression in their films.

218 S.[ilke], J.[ames]. "*High and Low.*" *Cinema* [Los Angeles], 1, no. 6 (November-December), 46.

   Favorable review. Focuses on "overall filmic action." Deals with the problem of evil.

219 _____. "*The Stray Dog.*" *Cinema* [Los Angeles], 1, no. 4, 46.

   Favorable review. Discusses the theme of good and evil, Kurosawa's humanity, and his belief in individual action. Says film "projects all the rugged beauty of an uncut gem."

220 Silke, James R. "Tetsugakusha, Kurosawa Akira" [Philosopher, Akira Kurosawa]. Trans. by Keigo Hirao. *Kinema Jumpo*, Special Issue, Kurosawa Akira: Sono Sakuhin to Kao [Akira Kurosawa: His Films and Face] (April), p. 79.

   Discusses Kurosawa's unique passion, beauty and style in his treatment of a new "Dark Age" in which the common people must face the turmoil by a corrupt government and business world.

221 Thompson, Howard. "*High and Low.*" *The New York Times* (27 November), p. 30.

   Favorable review on all accounts. Calls the film "one of the best detective thrillers ever filmed."

222 _____. "*The Idiot.*" *The New York Times* (1 May), p. 35.

   Adverse review of the first half of *The Idiot*, which he calls "loose" and "blurred," but refers to the second half as "a honey."

223 Yodogawa, Choji. "Kurosawa Gakko no Seito Tachi: Nihon Eiga no Shusai Zoroi" [Pupils of the Kurosawa School: A Line-Up of the Best in Japanese Movies]. *Kinema Jumpo*, Special Issue, Kurosawa Akira: Sono Sakuhin to Kao [Akira Kurosawa: His Films and Face] (April), pp. 74-78.

   High praise for all members of Kurosawa's school. Concludes that splendid, manly performances of all the actors are due to the masculine influence of Kurosawa and his scenario writers.

1964

224 Anon. "Notes." Trans. by Hiroko Kuroda. *Études cinématographique*, nos. 30-31 (Spring), pp. 115. First published by Toho Co., n.d.

225 Anon. "Seven Bullets." *Newsweek*, 63, no. 10 (9 March), 84.

   Favorable review of *Stray Dog*. Refers to the "purity of the obvious" and the "simplicity of surfaces."

226 Anon. "Tokyo Man Hunt." *Time*, 83, no. 11 (13 March), 101.

   Reserved review of *Stray Dog*. Sees the plot as a device to view postwar Japan. Mentions film's brilliant climax.

227 Anon. "*Stray Dog.*" *Filmfacts*, 7, p. 137.
Plot synopsis, credits, and excerpts from American reviewers.

228 "Akira Kurosawa." *Études cinématographiques*, nos. 30-31 (Spring), 128 pp.
Collection of eleven essays on Kurosawa, his work, and individual films, particularly *Rashomon, The Idiot, Ikiru, The Throne of Blood, The Hidden Fortress,* and *High and Low*. Authors include Chiyota Shimizu, Tadashi Iijima, Andre Labarrere, Barthélemy Amengual, Michel Estève, Philippe Handiquet, Claude Perrin, and Alberto Pesce.

229 Amengual, Barthélemy. "*Rashomon* ou la porte du démon de ... l'histoire." *Études cinématographiques*, nos. 30-31 (Spring), pp. 35-45.
Analyzes the mixture of theatricality and realism in *Rashomon* and the influence of Pirandello's concept of the relative nature of truth. Sees the result as a story of man's condition and ability to lie, rather than a metaphysical study of truth.

230 Beck, James M. "*Stray Dog.*" *Films in Review*, 15, no. 4 (April), 240-241.
Adverse review. Calls script "ridiculous" and refers to Kurosawa's work as "uneven."

231 Billard, Pierre. "*Un mervielleux dimanche.*" *Cinéma '64* [Paris], no. 83 (February), pp. 66-68.
Short analysis of *One Wonderful Sunday* in which Kurosawa shows the resilient human spirit during the ruin and misery of the postwar period. Discusses Kurosawa's use of startling images to symbolize man's confrontation with dreams, ideals, and reality.

232 Crowther, Bosley. "*Stray Dog.*" *The New York Times* (4 March), p. 32.
Reserved review. Considers it as a crude, early work with some "vivid, and poetic scenes."

233 Estève, Michel, ed. "Akira Kurosawa." *Études cinématographiques*, nos. 30-31 (Spring), 128 pp.
Collection of eleven essays on Kurosawa, his work, and individual films, particularly *Rashomon, The Idiot, Ikiru, The Throne of Blood, The Hidden Fortress,* and *High and Low*. Authors include Chiyota Shimizu, Tadashi Iizima, Andre Labarrere, Barthélemy Amengual, Michel Estève, Philippe Handiquet, Claude Perrin, and Albert Pesce.

234 _____. "*Hakuchi:* Une purete fascinante." *Études cinématographiques*, nos. 30-31 (Spring), pp. 50-54.
Compares Kurosawa's *The Idiot* with Lampin's French version and the Russian film of *Ivan Pyriev*. Considers Kurosawa's film most faithful to the spirit of Dostoyevsky's world, though the least faithful to the details of the novel. Feels Kurosawa universalized Dostoyevsky's work.

235 _____. "Le réalism de *Kumonosu-jo.*" *Études cinématographiques*, nos. 30-31 (Spring), pp. 66-74.
Comparison of *The Throne of Blood* with Orson Welles' *Macbeth*. Considers Kurosawa's film a key work, a powerful and poetic attempt to suggest the alienation

of a man who freely accepts the forces of evil. Feels film brings together the differing characters of Japan and England.

236 ———. "*Tengoku to Jigoku:* Une parabole du paradis perdu." *Études cinématographiques*, nos. 30-31 (Spring), pp. 83-89.

Analysis of *High and Low* in terms of two large movements of varying tempos. Sees first movement as slow and claustrophibic; the second as rapid and tense. Feels contrast creates dimension and suspense.

237 Ezratty, Sacha. *Kurosawa*. Classiques du cinéma, No. 15. Paris: Editions Universitaires, 186 pp.

Detailed biographical sketch, production notes, and background information for all films up to 1964 and filmography. Brief chronology of the Japanese cinema from 1896 to 1960, a chapter on the decline of the samurai, and one on Dostoyevsky, Shakespeare and Gorky. Book stresses Kurosawa's concern for contemporary problems and his interest in all human beings, not just those typically Japanese.

238 Gill, Brendan. "First Steps." *The New Yorker*, 40, no. 3 (7 March), 169-170.

Favorable review of *Stray Dog*. Plot outline. Lists recent successes of Mifune and Kurosawa.

239 Glazer, Nathan. "*The Seven Samurai*." *East-West Center Review*, 1 (July), 38-43.

Excellent article comparing *Seven Samurai* with the American adaptation, *The Magnificent Seven*. Focuses on how character is revealed, the importance of caste in the Japanese version, the use of Mexicans in the American version, and the social aspects of the American Western.

240 Handiquet, Philippe. "La tragédie de l'homme: *Ikiru*." *Études cinématographiques*, nos. 30-31 (Spring), pp. 55-65.

Analysis of the spiritual awakening in *Ikiru*. Sees personal tragedy as superimposed on society. Discusses Watanabe's realization of the uselessness of life.

241 Hirai, Yoshio. "Gamen ni Kage No nai Eiga wa Nai" [Every Movie Has Its Shadows]. *Kinema Jumpo* Special Issue, no. 10 (5 September), pp. 103-106.

Comments by Kurosawa collaborators. Reveals Kurosawa's desire for realistic swordplay (not achieved through tricky camera angles or cutting), and authentic decor and clothing. Examples given from several films.

242 Iijima Tadashi. "Akira Kurosawa." Trans. by Hiroko Kuroda. *Études cinématographiques*, nos. 30-31 (Spring), pp. 22-26. Extract from *Rétrospective du cinéma japonais*, 1963.

Analyzes the traits and characteristics of each period of Kurosawa's work: action films during the war, social dramas and historical films afterwards. Sees continuing trend of social significance.

243 ———. "*Hakuchi:* Une entreprise courageuse." *Études cinematographiques*, nos. 30-31 (Spring), pp. 46-49. First published in *Kinema Jumpo*, 1951.

Discussion of the difficulties of transposing Dostoyevsky's *The Idiot* to the screen and shifting the setting to Japan. Deals with the necessity of imposing an expressionistic character on the costumes, decor, and performances. Feels Kurosawa is unsuccessful in capturing the messianic nature of the novel and that Dostoyevsky's philosophic ideas remain imprecise and vague in the film, a result of the confusion of style and content.

244   Ishii, Kenneth. "Kurosawa Mifune ni Mono o Kiku" [Listening to Kurosawa and Mifune]. Trans. by Keigo Hirao. *Kinema Jumpo*, Special Issue, no. 10 (5 September), pp. 90-92.

Talks about the common trait of perfectionism in both Kurosawa and Mifune. Shows how Kurosawa elicits best performance from Mifune by long rehearsals and long, uncut sequences. Cites Kurosawa's preference for current projects when asked to name his favorite film.

245   J.[arvie], I.[an]. "High and Low." *Film*, no. 41, pp. 16-17.

Favorable review. Discusses the film's "bold," two-part structure. Calls the work "dazzling," a "bravura piece."

246   Kurosawa, Akira. "Notes à propos de mes films." *Études cinématographiques*, nos. 30-31 (Spring), pp. 12-21.

Kurosawa discusses each of his films individually and evaluates each in the totality of his work.

247   _____. "Why Mifune's Beard Won't Be Red." *Cinema* [Los Angeles], 2, no. 2 (July), 40.

Brief comment by Kurosawa on his rejection of color photography as too strong to capture the subdued colors so peculiarly Japanese.

248   Labarrere, Andre. "Un témoin du japon contemporain." *Études cinématographique*, nos. 30-31 (Spring), pp. 27-33.

Deals with Kurosawa's realism in both subject matter and treatment of material. Shows his primary concern for moral and social problems and his disregard for legend. Cites Ozu and Mizoguchi as representing traditional Japan; Kurosawa, modern Japan.

249   Mifune, Toshiro. "Mifune Toshiro wa Kataru: Satsuei Genba de Jitakude Shaberu Akahige to yu Otoko no Hanashi" [Mifune Talks: A Story of a Man Called Red Beard]. *Kinema Jumpo*, Special Issue, no. 10 (5 September), pp. 93-95.

Documents the exhausting work of making a Kurosawa film, and special pressures resulting from Kurosawa's fondness for long takes. Notes Kurosawa's method of checking each set-up when using multiple cameras. Discusses the sense of group responsibility.

250   Perrin, Claude. "Un épopée sociale: *Kakushi Toride no San-Akunin.*" *Études cinématographiques*, nos. 30-31 (Spring), pp. 75-78.

Sees *The Hidden Fortress* as part of Kurosawa's continuing concern with struggle and conflict. Characterizes film as surreal, a nightmare. Considers Kurosawa's animated landscape, the rugged mountains, and the unbearable heat as symbols for the universal violence which dominates man.

251 Pesce, Alberto. "Tengoku to Jigoku: Un recit en six actes." *Études cinématographiques*, nos. 30-31 (Spring), pp. 79-82.

Discusses *High and Low* as an American inspired detective story presented in six acts. Shows how Kurosawa sets up a stratification of forms and styles which exemplify the various linguistic traditions of the cinema.

252 Richie, Donald. "Kurosawa on Kurosawa." *Sight and Sound*, 33, nos. 3 and 4 (Summer and Autumn), 108-113 and 200-203. Reprinted in *Interviews With Film Directors*, 1967 and *Kurosawa*, n.d. (**466**).

Comments by Kurosawa on all his films from *Sanshiro Sugata*, to *Sanjuro*. Includes personal memories of filming, relationship with actors and crew, problems during production, preferences, and information on personal life.

252a Sarris, Andrew. "Films." *The Village Voice* (15 October), p. 14.

Review of *The Outrage*, a remake of *Rashomon*. Claims *Rashomon* is better in every way, but that both films are fallacious. Reevaluation of Kurosawa. Feels his works contain an "almost obsessive misanthropy coupled with selective sentimentality." Sees *Rashomon* not as four stories which present subjective truth, but as four lies. Calls both films muddled.

253 Sherwin, Sally. "*Stray Dog.*" *Film Comment*, 2, no. 1 (Winter), 38-39.

Review of film. Feels work structurally flawed, but still intriguing.

254 Shimizu, Chiyota. "Entretien avec Akira Kurosawa." Trans. by Hiroko Kuroda. *Études cinématographique*, nos. 30-31 (Spring), pp. 3-11. First published in *Kinema Jumpo*, 1952-1953.

Kurosawa discusses his interest in Dostoyevsky, the process of adapting literary works to the screen, and why few women have principal roles in his films. States Toho against revealing women's faults on the screen for fear of displeasing audiences.

255 Sugimura, Haruko, Kyoko Kagawa, Miyuki Kuwano, Akemi Negishi and Reiko Dan. "Onna no Mede Mita Futari no Otoko" [Two Men (Kurosawa and Mifune) Seen through the Eyes of Women]. *Kinema Jumpo*, Special Issue (5 September), pp. 107-111.

All the women agree that despite Kurosawa's reputation as a tyrant, he is gentle and encouraging to actors.

256 Takeda, Taijun. "Futarino Nihonjin So" [Thinking of Two Japanese.] *Kinema Jumpo* Special Issue (5 September), pp. 64-67.

Takeda, a novelist, proposes a thorough research into the elements of "Japaneseness" and "manliness" as evidenced by Kurosawa and Mifune in Kurosawa films. Believes the team was born from shared hardships within the Japanese movie industry.

1965

257 Anon. "Akira Kurosawa." *The East*, 1, no. 6 (July), 45-49.

Detailed biography of Kurosawa from childhood through early film career. Comments on *Red Beard*.

258 Anon. "Kurosawa, Akira," in *Current Biography*. New York: H.W. Wilson, p. 27.

Biographical information. Brief discussion of important films. Includes quotations from Kurosawa and several film critics.

259 Anon. "Probing for Kurosawa's Secret: Symposium." *Atlas*, 9, no. 299 (May), 299-301. Trans. from *Chuo Koron*, Tokyo.

Discussion between scenarist Kikushima, critic Iwasaki and reporter Kusakabe on development of Kurosawa's style and thinking from *Stray Dog* to *High and Low*. Comparison of the two films.

260 Blumenthal, J.[erry]. "*Macbeth* into *Throne of Blood*." *Sight and Sound*, 34, no. 4 (Autumn), pp. 190-195. Reprinted in *Film and the Liberal Arts*, 1970, *Renaissance of the Film*, 1970, and *Film Theory and Criticism*, 1974.

Deals with Kurosawa's adaptation of Shakespeare's play. Shows how Kurosawa found visual equivalents for Shakespeare's language and interiority in film imagery and setting. Demonstrates how Kurosawa avoided theatricality inappropriate to the film medium. Special attention to the setting, the forest, and characterizations.

261 Brook, Peter. "Shakespeare on Three Screens." *Sight and Sound*, 34, no. 2 (Spring), p. 68.

Brief mention of *The Throne of Blood*, but calls the film the best adaptation of Shakespeare on the screen.

262 C.[rawford], S.[tanley]. *Red Beard. Film*, no. 44 (Winter), pp. 16-17.

Mixed reactions with some disappointments. But praise for Kurosawa's use of the wide screen.

263 Hawk. "*Akahige (Red Beard)*," *Variety* (8 September), p. 6.

Adverse review. Calls film "hokum lifted to the highest denominator." Also feels film is too long.

264 Higham, Charles. "Kurosawa's Humanism." *Kenyon Review*, 27, no. 4 (Autumn), 737-742.

Discusses film from *Judo Saga* through masterpieces *The Bad Sleep Well* and *High and Low*. Talks about the influence of Ford, Stevens, and Wyler on Kurosawa's work. Notes "austere beauty" and "splendor of the body" in films like *Rashomon*. Refers to Kurosawa's humanity for all but the inhuman.

265 Iwasaki, Akira. "Kurosawa and His Work." *Japan Quarterly*, 12, no. 1 (January-March), 59-64. Reprinted in *Focus on Rashomon*, 1972.

Discusses how Kurosawa's work reflects the blending of East and West. Calls Kurosawa a "perfectionist" filmmaker. Shows his interest in "unconventional" and "startling" ways to tell a story. Refers to Kurosawa's intellectual conception of plot, character and setting. Special focus on *Rashomon*. Notes how Kurosawa differs from other Japanese directors.

266 Kael, Pauline. "*Yojimbo*," in *I Lost It at the Movies*. Boston: Little Brown, pp. 239-245. First published in *The Partisan Review*, 1963.

267 MacDonald, Dwight. "Films." *Esquire* (December), p. 84.

Adverse review of *Red Beard*. Takes issue with Richard Roud's evaluation of the film. Calls the work "banal and sentimental."

*268 Ortolani, Benito. "Films and Faces of Akira Kurosawa." *America*, 113 (2 October), 368-371.
    Cited in Schuster, Mel. *Motion Picture Directors: A Bibliography of Magazine and Periodical Articles, 1900-1972*, Metuchen, N.J.: Scarecrow, 1973, p. 230.

269 Richie, Donald. *The Films of Akira Kurosawa*. Berkeley: University of California Press, 218 pp. Second edition, 1970.
    Most complete work on Kurosawa in English. Detailed plot synopsis and analysis of each film up through *Red Beard*. Extensive production information. Generous quotations from the scenarios. Essay on Kurosawa's method, technique, and style. Complete filmography and a selective bibliography.

270 _____. "Red Beard." *Film Quarterly*, 19, no. 1 (Fall), pp. 14-25.
    Abridged version of the chapter in Richie's full-length book on Kurosawa. Treats story, characterization, treatment, and production. Calls film the story of "an education." Compares characters in *Red Beard* with heroes and villains in other Kurosawa films. Deals with the use of sound.

271 Sadoul, Georges. "Au Japon: Akira Kurosawa et Georges Sadoul." *Cinema '65* [Paris], no. 92 (January), pp. 75-83.
    Conversation between Sadoul and Kurosawa on filming techniques (especially multiple cameras), the commercial aspects of film-making in Japan (short production schedules) and the constraining influence of foreign culture on Japanese art forms in the postwar era.

272 Sato, Tadao. "Sengo Eiga Towa Nanika? Kurosawa Akira to Shakaishugi Eiga" [What is the Post-war Film? — Akira Kurosawa and Socialist Movies]. *Eiga Geijutsu* (December), pp. 47-50.
    Opposes Iwasaki's view that postwar movies like *Rashomon* opened the door to a new era in Japanese movies because of their despair and mistrust of humanity and objective truth. Sato sees them rather as a rethinking of the ego which is characteristic of the postwar literature which blossomed once governmental restrictions were lifted.

273 Silverstein, Norman. "Kurosawa's Detective-Story Parables." *Japan Quarterly*, 13, no. 3 (July-September), 351-354.
    Deals with Kurosawa's films as moral allegories of man's struggle between good and evil, especially in *Stray Dog* and *High and Low*. Shows Kurosawa's Christian belief in the triumph of good over evil through man's determination to do good. Calls films "morally instructive." Also details changes in adapting *King's Ransom* to screen for *High and Low*.

274 T.[ailleur], R.[oger]. "Akahige (Barberousse), d'Akira Kurosawa (Japon)." *Positif*, no. 72 (December-January), pp. 9-10.
    Refers to *Red Beard* as "inspired," "a monumental fresco." Refers to its winning of the prize of the Catholic Office.

*275 Thomas, John. "Yojimbo." *A.F.F.S. Newsletter* (February), pp. 17-18.
    Cited in Batty, Linda. *Retrospective Index to Film Periodicals, 1930-1971*. New York: R. R. Bowker, 1975, p. 194.

1966

276 Bucher, Felix. "Akira Kurosawa — Hiroshi Teshigahara." *Camera 45*, no. 9 (September), pp. 50-55.
Talks of Kurosawa's rejection of "artless simplicity" typical of most Japanese film and debates issue of how Western Kurosawa is.

277 Cowie, Peter, ed. "Akira Kurosawa," in *International Film Guide, 1966*. London: Tantivy Press; New York: A.S. Barnes, pp. 13-17.
Brief comments of Kurosawa's life, films and major themes. Cowie calls him a man of all genres and a complete *auteur*. Filmography includes credits from *Sanshiro Sugata* through *Red Beard*.

278 Gadi, R.B. "An Afternoon with Kurosawa." *Solidarity*, 1, no. 1 (January-March), 57-63. Reprinted in *Focus on Rashomon*, 1972.
Discusses Kurosawa as a moral director, whose films reflect the plight of Japan and Asia. Discusses several of Kurosawa's adaptations for the screen.

279 Kauffmann, Stanley. *"Ikiru," "Throne of Blood," "The Hidden Fortress; The Lower Depths," "Yojimbo," "Sanjuro," "The Bad Sleep Well,"* and *"High and Low,"* in *A World of Film: Criticism and Comment*. New York: Harper & Row, pp. 374-385. First published in *The New Republic*, 1960, 1961, 1962, 1963.

280 Mesnil, Michel. "Visite á l'empereur du Japon: Un entretien avec Akira Kurosawa." *Cinema '66* [Paris], no. 103 (February), pp. 50-64.
An interview in which Kurosawa discusses politics. Claims themes in his films emerge naturally and are not the result of fixed political commitments. Discusses his desire to show the profound misery which lies beneath the facade of prosperity in contemporary Japan. Notes two tendencies in his works: the realistic and the artistic. Feels that he takes only the best aspects of foreign films whereas most young Japanese filmmakers blindly imitate Western trends.

281 Richie, Donald. *The Japanese Movie: An Illustrated History*. Tokyo: Kodansha International, passim.
Social history of the Japanese cinema from beginnings in 1894. Touches on Kurosawa's works. Profusely illustrated.

282 Shirai, Yoshio, Hayao Shibata and Koichi Yamada. "L'Empereur: Entretien avec Kurosawa." *Cahiers du cinéma*, no. 182, pp. 34-42, 74.
Interview in which Kurosawa explains why he switches from historical to modern settings. "The advantage of historical films comes from the spectacular elements they offer, like adventure, which is an essential motif of the cinema." Kurosawa talks of his love for Westerns and Russian literature and their influence on his work, censorship problems during and after the war, scenario writing, and his use of Mifune and other actors in 'the Kurosawa family.'

283 Thompson, Howard. "Kurosawa to Make Film Jointly With Embassy Pictures." *The New York Times* (1 July), p. 42.
Discusses the deal for Kurosawa's first color film in the U.S., *The Runaway Train*.

284 Yamada, Koichi. "Biofilmographie de Kurosawa Akira." *Cahiers du cinéma*, no. 182 (September), pp. 50-51, 78.
   Complete filmography through 1951 (*The Idiot*).

285 _____. "Destin de Samourai." *Cahiers du cinema*, no. 182 (September), pp. 44-49.
   An analysis of the samurai hero in Kurosawa films — the image of the great man who does great deeds. Discusses the hierarchical code which prevents peasants from acting as heroes. Notes the idealization of the samurai in contrast to Kurosawa's realistic treatment of the peasants. Investigates the effect of the war on Kurosawa's films and the blurred oppositions in the postwar period which depict a time where the mission of the samurai has ended.

1967

286 Anon. "*I Live in Fear*." *Filmfacts*, 10, p. 33.
   Plot synopsis, credits, and excerpts from American reviewers.

287 "Akira Kurosawa: Japan's Poet Laureate of Film," in *Film Makers on Film Making*. Edited by Harry M. Geduld. Bloomington: Indiana University Press, pp. 271-275. First published in *Show Business Illustrated*, 1962, see entry no. 168.

288 Crowther, Bosley. "*I Live in Fear*." *The New York Times* (29 January), p. 25.
   Reserved review. Finds the film "one of the weakest of the great Japanese director's work."

289 _____. "Rasho-mon," in *The Great Films: Fifty Golden Years of Motion Pictures*. New York: G.P. Putnam's Sons, pp. 202-206.
   Comments on the film's reception in Japan and in Venice. Lengthy plot summary and critical comments.

290 Ezratty, Sacha. "Kurosawa Akira Ron" [Akira Kurosawa Theory], in *Sekai no Eiga Sakka — Kurosawa Akira* [*Film Directors of the World — Akira Kurosawa*], No. 3. Tokyo: Kinema Jumpo Sha, pp. 131-142.
   Emphasizes Kurosawa's interest in current problems. States that his films do not merely create "typical Japanese," but rather human beings. Therefore feels he is a great humanist as well as a great filmmaker.

291 Hartung, Philip T. "The Screen." *The Commonweal*, 85, no. 19 (17 February), 565-567.
   Favorable review of *I Live in Fear*. Plot synopsis.

292 M., J. "What Happened to Earth?" *Newsweek*, 69, no. 6 (February), 97.
   Mixed review. Calls film "shaky" but still more interesting than works by lesser directors. Sees Japan's continuing obsession and fear of radioactive fallout.

293 Pinto, Alfonso. "Akira Kurosawa." *Films in Review*, 18, no. 4 (April), 255.
   Filmography through 1965.

294 Richie, Donald. "Akira Kurosawa." *Interview with Film Directors.* Edited by Andrew Sarris. New York: Avon Books, pp. 287-308. First published in *Sight and Sound,* 1964.
Interviews include added editorial comments by Sarris.

*295 Sesonske, Alexander. "Throne of Blood." *Film Society Review* (February), pp. 25-27.
Cited in Batty, Linda. *Retrospective Index to Film Periodicals 1930-1971.* New York: R. R. Bowker, 1975, p. 91.

296 Tyler, Parker. "*Rashomon* as Modern Art," in *Three Faces of the Film.* Cranbury, N.J.: A.S. Barnes, pp. 36-43. First published in *Cinema 16,* 1952.

297 Vas, Robert. "High and Low." *Sight and Sound,* 36, no. 3 (Summer), 149.
Treatment of work as three separate films.

1968

298 Anon. "Red Beard." *Filmfacts,* 11, p. 516.
Plot synopsis, credits, and excerpts from American reviewers.

299 Crist, Judith. "87th Precinct — Japanese Style," in *The Private Eye, the Cowboy and the Very Naked Girl.* Chicago: Holt, Rinehart and Winston, pp. 36-39. First printed in *The New York Herald Tribune,* 1963.

300 Kurosawa, Akira, Shinobu Hashimoto and Hideo Oguni. *Ikiru.* Edited by Donald Richie. New York: Simon and Schuster, 88 pp.
Complete screenplay and credits. Also photographs and filmography through 1965. Introductory essay by Richie emphasizes Watanabe's discovery of self through action. Discusses existential philosophy and the stripping away of illusions in *Ikiru.*

301 Sato, Tadao. *Kurosawa Akira no Sekai* [*The World of Akira Kurosawa*]. Tokyo: Sanichi Shobo Company, 299 pp.
Treats the works of Kurosawa from his earliest scenarios, directed by others, through *Red Beard* (1965). Stresses relevant themes for a Japanese audience in the postwar period of spiritual depression. Emphasizes the need to face and fight against social problems. Probably the first analytic work devoted to one filmmaker written by a Japanese critic.

302 Thompson, Howard. "Red Beard." *The New York Times* (20 December), p. 60.
Reserved review. Finds the film long, slow and clichéd.

1969

303 Anon. "Epic Vision." *Time,* 93, no. 3 (17 January), 67.
Review of *Red Beard.* Slight admiration for the plot, but praises Kurosawa's treatment. Plot summary.

304 Bobker, Lee R. *Elements of Film.* New York: Harcourt, Brace and World, pp. 219-220.
Brief comments on Kurosawa's style, especially stylized storytelling, use of historical settings, emphasis on physical action, and expressive, mobile camera.

305 Davidson, James F. "Memory of Defeat in Japan: A Reappraisal of *Rashomon*," in *Rashomon: A Film by Akira Kurosawa.* Edited by Donald Richie. New York: Grove Press, pp. 209-221. First published in *The Antioch Review,* 1954.

306 Davis, Richard. "*Red Beard.*" *Films and Filming,* 15, no. 5 (February), p. 46.
Favorable review. Claims that Kurosawa takes a "popular formula" and creates a "near work of art."

307 Hall, Peter, "*Throne of Blood.*" *The London Times* (26 January), p. 113.
Calls work the most successful Shakesperean film ever made.

308 Kauffmann, Stanley. "True and Otherwise." *The New Republic,* 160, no. 2 (11 January), 20. Reprinted in *Figures of Light,* 1971.
Praise for Kurosawa and the actors for *Red Beard* but calls the script "dreadful."

309 Kurosawa, Akira and Shinobu Hashimoto. *Rashomon.* Edited and trans. by Donald Richie. New York: Grove Press, 256 pp.
Full screenplay, plus credits and over 200 frame enlargements. Two short stories by Ryunosuke Akutagawa on which the film was based. Three essays — an aesthetic analysis by Parker Tyler, social background by James F. Davidson, and production information by Donald Richie. Also includes an excerpt from MGM's adaptation *The Outrage.*

310 MacDonald, Dwight. "*The Hidden Fortress,*" "*Throne of Blood,*" and "*Yojimbo,*" in *On Movies.* Englewood Cliffs, N.J.: Prentice-Hall, pp. 419-422. First published in *Esquire,* 1961, 1962.

311 Richie, Donald. "Dostoevsky with a Japanese Camera," in *The Emergence of Film Art.* Edited by Lewis Jacobs. New York: Hopkinson and Blake, pp. 328-335. First published in *Horizon,* 1962.

312 ———. "*Rashomon* and Kurosawa," in *Rashomon: A Film by Akira Kurosawa.* Edited by Donald Richie. New York: Grove Press, pp. 222-240. First published as "*Rashomon,*" in *The Films of Akira Kurosawa,* 1965.
Reprint of chapter in Richie's own book on Kurosawa. Treats the source, the story, and production.

313 Tyler, Parker. "*Rashomon* as Modern Art," in *Rashomon: A Film by Akira Kurosawa.* Edited by Donald Richie. New York: Grove Press, pp. 195-208. First published in *Cinema 16,* 1952.

314 Wissink, Charles Van. "*Stray Dog,*" Program Notes, in *The Art of the Film,* Series No. 71, Program No. 3. Chicago: Roosevelt University Film

Society (30 April).
Historical background on the Japanese cinema, biographical information on Kurosawa and his films, comments on the actors and a critique of the film.

1970

315 Blumenthal, J.[erry]. "*Macbeth* into *Throne of Blood*," in *Film and the Liberal Arts*. Edited by T.J. Ross. New York: Holt, Rinehart & Winston, pp. 122-133. First published in *Sight and Sound*, 1965.

316 _____. "*Throne of Blood*," in *Renaissance of the Film*. Edited by Julius Bellone. London: Collier-MacMillan, pp. 289-305. First published in *Sight and Sound*, 1965.

317 Chekhonin, B. "A Few Stones From a Glass House: Kurosawa's Troubles in Big Bad Hollywood." *Atlas*, 19, no. 3 (March), 59-61.
Chronicles Kurosawa's move from Japan to Hollywood where he hoped to find greater artistic freedom. Gives background on *The Mad Locomotive* and *Tora! Tora! Tora!* Discusses disillusionment and belief in independent production.

318 Gillett, John. "Coca-Cola and the Golden Pavillion." *Sight and Sound*, 39 (Summer), 153-156.
Brief note on *Dodeskaden* during second day of shooting. Detailed information on financing.

319 Gow, Gordon. "*Yojimbo*." *Films and Filming*, 16, no. 11 (August), 46.
Reserved review. Plot summary.

320 Iwasaki, Akira. "Kurosawa Akira no Sekai" [The World of Akira Kurosawa], in *Sekai no Eiga Sakka — Kurosawa Akira* [*Film Directors of the World — Akira Kurosawa*], No. 3. Tokyo: Kinema Jumpo Sha., pp. 55-70.
Contrasts the European attitude to Kurosawa's films (too Westernized) with the American response (highly stimulating and enjoyable). Points out that Americans are little concerned with whether or not the films genuinely reflect Japanese characteristics.

321 Kofujita, Chieko, ed. *Sekai no Eiga Sakka — Kurosawa Akira* [*Film Directors of the World — Akira Kurosawa*], No. 3. Tokyo: Kinema Jumpo Sha., 238 pp.
Collection of ten critical essays on Kurosawa, a transcript of a panel discussion by Japanese film critics, and recollections by Kurosawa on his work. Also includes a complete scenario for *Snow*, written in 1947. Authors anthologized include: Sacha Ezratty, Akira Iwasaki, Yoichi Matsue, Teruyo Nogami, Tadao Sato, Yukichi Shinoda, Yoshio Shirai, Rikiya Tayama, Naoki Togawa and Kikuo Yamamoto.

322 Kurosawa, Akira. *The Seven Samurai*. Trans. by Donald Richie. New York: Simon and Schuster, 224 pp.
Introduction by Richie reprinted from his *The Films of Akira Kurosawa*. Full screen play, plus credits and photographs.

323   Matsue, Yoichi. "Kurosawa Akira: Sono Ningen, No. 2" [Akira Kurosawa: The Man] in *Sekai no Eiga Sakka — Kurosawa Akira* [*Film Directors of the World — Akira Kurosawa*], No. 3. Tokyo: Kinema Jump Sha., pp. 81-90.
Refers to films as Kurosawa's sole means of questioning the human condition.

324   Mosk, "*Dodeska-den.*" *Variety* (9 December).
Although the critic feels some may find the film "old hat," he thinks the work is "rousing" and "generally beguiling," a fine comeback for the director.

325   *The New York Times Film Reviews.* New York: Arno Press and New York Times Company, vols. 4-6.
Reprints of all reviews previously published in *The New York Times.*

326   Nogami, Teruyo. "Kurosawa Akira: Sono Ningen" [Akira Kurosawa: The Man], in *Sekai no Eiga Sakka — Kurosawa Akira* [*Film Directors of the World — Akira Kurosawa*], No. 3. Tokyo: Kinema Jumpo Sha., pp. 92-94.
Describes Kurosawa's habit of shouting on the set as a means of creating excitement. Tells how staff accept this as part of the work.

327   Richie, Donald. *The Films of Akira Kurosawa.* Berkeley: University of California Press, 223 pp., 2nd ed. First published in 1965.

328   _____. "Introduction," in *The Seven Samurai: A Film by Akira Kurosawa.* New York: Simon and Schuster, pp. 5-21. First published as "The Seven Samurai," in *The Films of Akira Kurosawa*, 1965.
Reprint of chapter in Richie's own book. Deals with the story, treatment, and production. Includes excerpts. Emphasis on Kurosawa's re-creation of the past, realism, creative cutting, use of motion, and the beauty of the images.

329   Sato, Tadao. "Kurosawa Akira no Eikyo" [Influences of Akira Kurosawa], in *Sekai no Eiga Sakka — Kurosawa Akira* [*Film Directors of the World — Akira Kurosawa*], No. 3. Tokyo: Kinema Jumpo Sha., pp. 95-104.
Comments on the tendency of other filmmakers to borrow from Kurosawa, ironically copying the superficial aspects of his work and not the essential elements.

330   Shimaji, Takamaro, ed. *Dodeskaden*, in *Kurosawa Akira Eiga Taikei* [*Complete Works of Akira Kurosawa*], No. 1. Tokyo: Kinema Jumpo Sha., 138 pp.
Complete screenplay in both English and Japanese for *Dodeskaden*, with small stills of each shot. Includes a detailed diary (in Japanese only) which discusses the hardships of handling children and problems of color. Essays by Tadao Sato (in Japanese only) on the structure of the film.

331   _____, ed. *Kurosawa Akira Eiga Taikei* [*Complete Works of Akira Kurosawa*]. Tokyo: Kinema Jumpo Sha., 12 vols.
A series of twelve volumes, to be published over a period of years, which provide scenarios (dialogue, plus technical information) for all Kurosawa works, in both Japanese and English, plus small stills of each shot. To date only vols. 1-4, 6, and 9 have appeared. Volumes include: 1. *Dodeskaden.* Takamaro Shimaji, ed., 1970. 2. *Sanshiro Sugata* and *No Regrets For Our Youth.* Kimi Aida, trans., 1971. 3. *One*

Wonderful Sunday and *Drunken Angel*. Don Kenny, trans., 1971. 4. *The Quiet Duel* and *Stray Dog*. Don Kenny, trans., 1971. 6. *The Idiot* and *To Live*. Don Kenny, trans., 1971. 9. *Three Badmen in a Hidden Fortress* and *The Bad Sleep Well*. Don Kenny, trans., 1971.

332   no entry.

333   Shinoda, Yukichi. "Kurosawa Eiga o Sasaeru Hitobito" [The People Who Support the Films of Kurosawa], in *Sekai no Eiga Sakka — Kurosawa Akira* [*Film Directors of the World — Akira Kurosawa*], No. 3. Tokyo: Kinema Jumpo Sha., pp. 187-194.

Bemoans Kurosawa's long silence since *Red Beard*. Refers to him as an unhappy "giant," who needs understanding and support. Also points out the existence of other "giants" within the Kurosawa team.

334   Shirai, Yoshio. "Kurosawa Akira: Sono Ningen, No. 1" [Akira Kurosawa: The Man], in *Sekai no Eiga Sakka — Kurosawa Akira* [*Film Directors of the World — Akira Kurosawa*], No. 3. Tokyo: Kinema Jumpo Sha., pp. 71-80.

Documents the responses of Kurosawa during filming.

335   Strick, Philip. "*Dodeskaden*." *Sight and Sound*, 40, no. 1 (Winter), 18.

Favorable review. Deals with the use of color and symbolism and the dreams of individual characters.

336   Tayama, Rikiya. "Kaigai no Kurosawa Akira Ron" [Interpretation of Akira Kurosawa Abroad], in *Sekai no Eiga Sakka — Kurosawa Akira* [*Film Directors of the World — Akira Kurosawa*], No. 3. Tokyo: Kinema Jumpo Sha., pp. 123-130.

Discusses the increasing appearance of detailed analysis and criticism of Kurosawa's work appearing in overseas journals and newspapers.

337   Togawa, Naoki. "Kurosawa Akira no Shikaku Gengo" [The Visual Language of Akira Kurosawa], in *Sekai no Eiga Sakka — Kurosawa Akira* [*Film Directors of the World — Akira Kurosawa*], No. 3. Tokyo: Kinema Jumpo Sha., pp. 105-112.

Describes Kurosawa as a very romantic person whose tendency is to simplify description. Notes that all of Kurosawa's films deal with the common people. Calls this the secret of his power.

338   Tyler, Parker. "*Rashomon* as Modern Art," in *Renaissance of the Film*. Edited by Julius Bellone. London: Collier-MacMillan, pp. 198-210. First published in *Cinema 16*, 1952.

339   Yamamoto, Kikuo. "Kurosawa Akira Ron no Shiteki Tembo" [An Historical View of Akira Kurosawa], in *Sekai no Eiga Sakka — Kurosawa Akira* [*Film Directors of the World — Akira Kurosawa*], No. 3. Tokyo: Kinema Jumpo Sha., pp. 113-122.

Discusses the importance of Tadao Sato's full-length study of Kurosawa and points out the need for similar studies on Ozu and Mizoguchi.

1971

340 Aida, Kimi, trans. *Sanshiro Sugata* [*Sugata Sanshiro*] and *No Regrets for Our Youth* [*Waga Seishun ni Kuinashi*], in *Complete Works of Akira Kurosawa* [*Kurosawa Akira Eiga Taikei*], No. 2. Tokyo: Kinema Jumpo Sha., 136 pp.

Complete scenarios in both Japanese and English plus small stills for each shot. Complete credits.

341 Callenbach, Ernest. "Short Notices." *Film Quarterly*, 24, no. 4 (Summer), 63.

Short review and plot summary of *Dodeskaden*. Notes picaresque structure. States film "takes place in the country of an old man's mind."

342 Clurman, Harold. "Theatre and Films." *The Nation*, 213, no. 14 (1 November), 446.

Reserved review of *Dodeskaden*, but refers to the film's "cruel realism." Brief plot and theme summation.

343 Cohn, Bernard. "Un humaniste sceptique (sur *Dodeskaden*)." *Positif*, no. 132 (December), pp. 56-58.

Calls the film a summation and extension of Kurosawa's social themes. Refers to the "mosaic of portraits" which treats each character in detail and never appears condescending. Compares Kurosawa to Gorky and Dostoyevsky in his development of psychological depth.

344 Crowdus, Gary. *Dodeska-Den*." *Film Society Review*, 7, no. 3 (November), 20.

Brief note on the film.

345 Gow, Gordon. "*Sanjuro*." *Films and Filming*, 17, no. 4 (January), 56.

Favorable review, especially for Mifune's performance and the film's humor.

346 Greenspun, Roger. "Film Fete: Lives in a Junk Yard in Kurosawa's *Dodeskaden*." *The New York Times* (6 October), p. 39.

Adverse review. Finds the "humor strained" and feels the film was "artificially produced."

347 Henry, Jim. "Kurosawa Urges Younger Pic Execs, Govt. Loans to Save Japan's Film Biz." *Variety* (17 February), p. 30.

Kurosawa states need to save Japan's dying film industry by rejuvenating top management of all major film companies and by obtaining government loans. Also urges companies to distribute independent productions.

348 Kenny, Don, trans. *The Idiot* [*Hakuchi*] and *To Live* [*Ikiru*] in *Complete Works of Akira Kurosawa* [*Kurosawa Akira Eiga Taikei*], No. 6, Tokyo: Kinema Jumpo Sha., 192 pp.

Complete scenarios in both Japanese and English plus small stills for each shot. Complete credits.

349 _____, trans. *One Wonderful Sunday* [Subarashiki Nichiyobi] and *Drunken Angel* [*Yoidore Tenshi*], in *Complete Works of Akira Kurosawa* [*Kurosawa Akira Eiga Taikei*], No. 3. Tokyo: Kinema Jumpo Sha., 136 pp.

Complete scenarios in both Japanese and English and small stills for each shot. Complete credits.

350 _____, trans. *The Quiet Duel* [*Shizukanaru Ketto* and *Stray Dog* [*Nora Inu*], in *Complete Works of Akira Kurosawa* [*Kurosawa Akira Eiga Takei*], No. 4. Tokyo: Kinema Jumpo Sha., 168 pp.

Complete scenarios in both Japanese and English and small stills for each shot. Complete credits.

351 _____, trans. *Three Badmen in a Hidden Fortress* [*Kakushi Toride no San-Akunin*] and *The Bad Sleep Well* [*Warui Yatsu Hodo Yoku Nemuru*], in *Complete Works of Akira Kurosawa* [*Kurosawa Akira Eiga Takei*], No. 9. Tokyo: Kinema Jumpo Sha., 248 pp.

Complete scenarios in both Japanese and English and small stills for each shot. Complete credits.

352 Kurosawa, Akira. "Dits." *Positif*, no. 132 (December) pp. 46-50.

The interview covers comments on abandoned projects; his multiple camera technique; special effects, especially in *Red Beard*; his collaboration with composers; his repertory acting company; political influences; and the influence of the Noh theater.

353 Manvell, Roger. "Akira Kurosawa's *Macbeth*, *The Castle of the Spider's Web*," in *Shakespeare and the Film*. London: J.M. Dent & Sons, pp. 101-113.

General background on *The Throne of Blood*. Includes a long excerpt from an interview by Tadao Sato with Kurosawa on the influence of Noh drama on the film, an extract of the murder scene from the film script a synopsis of an article by J. Blumenthal, and an outline of the work. Calls the film "a distillation," not an adaptation.

354 Niogret, Hubert. "Notes sur quelques films de Kurosawa." *Positif*, no. 132 (December), pp. 51-55.

Discusses eight films covering Kurosawa's career from 1943 to 1963. Places films in a social and political context. Treats Kurosawa's contribution to the Japanese war effort (which he disowns today), relevant themes, humor, and his development of dramatic situation and atmosphere.

355 Richie, Donald. *Japanese Cinema: Film Style and National Character.* Garden City, NY: Doubleday & Company, pp. 197-237 and passim. First published as *Japanese Movies*, 1961.

356 Svenson, Arne. "Kurosawa, Akira" in *Japan*. London: A. Zwemmer; New York: A.S. Barnes & Co., pp. 55-56.

Gives biographical information on the director and a complete filmography, including Kurosawa's screen credits as a scriptwriter for other directors. Book also includes credits, plot descriptions and commentary for some of Kurosawa's most important works.

1972

*357   Anon. "Director's Decline." *Japanese Fantasy Film Journal*, 9.
Cited in Schuster, Mel. *Motion Picture Directors: A Bibliography of Magazine and Periodical Articles, 1900-1972*. Metuchen, N.J.: 1973, p. 230.

358   Anon. "Rashomon," in *Focus on Rashomon*. Edited by Donald S. Richie. Englewood Cliffs, N.J.: Prentice-Hall, pp. 41-42. First published in *Time*, 1952.

359   Barbarow, George. "*Rashomon* and the Fifth Witness," in *Focus on Rashomon*. Edited by Donald S. Richie. Englewood Cliffs, N.J.: Prentice-Hall, pp.65-68. First published in *The Hudson Review*, 1952.

360   Beaufort, John. "*Rashomon*," in *Focus on Rashomon*. Edited by Donald S. Richie. Englewood Cliffs, New Jersey: Prentice-Hall, pp. 38-40. First published in *The Christian Science Monitor*, 1952.

361   Crowther, Bosley. "*Rashomon*," in *Focus on Rashomon*. Edited by Donald S. Richie. Englewood Cliffs, New Jersey: Prentice-Hall, pp. 45-46. First published in *The New York Times*, 1952.

362   _____. "*Rashomon*," in *Focus on Rashomon*. Edited by Donald S. Richie. Englewood Cliffs, New Jersey: Prentice-Hall, pp. 43-45. First published in *The New York Times*, 1951.

363   Davidson, James F. "Memory of Defeat in Japan: A Reappraisal of *Rashomon*," in *Focus on Rashomon*. Edited by Donald S. Richie. Englewood Cliffs, New Jersey: Prentice-Hall, pp. 119-128. First published in *The Antioch Review*, 1954.

364   Farber, Manny. "*Rashomon*," in *Focus on Rashomon*. Edited by Donald S. Richie. Englewood Cliffs, New Jersey: Prentice-Hall, p. 47. First published in *The Nation*, 1952.

365   G., J. "Kurosawa Akira," in *The International Encyclopedia of Film*. Edited by Dr. Roger Manvell. New York: Crown Publishers, p. 324.
Critical evaluation of Kurosawa's career. Calls him the best-known Japanese director and refers to his "virtuoso style." Ultimately ranks him below Mizoguchi and Ozu because of his "trite symbolism and drawn-out sentimentality."

366   Gadi, R.B. "An Afternoon with Kurosawa," in *Focus on Rashomon*. Edited by Donald S. Richie. Englewood Cliffs, New Jersey: Prentice-Hall, pp. 8-20. First published in *Solidarity*, 1966.

367   Ghelli, Nino. "*Rashomon*," trans. by Robert M. Connolly, in *Focus on Rashomon*. Edited by Donald S. Richie. Englewood Cliffs, New Jersey:

Prentice-Hall, pp. 103-109. First published in *Bianco e Nero*, 13, no. 3, March, 1952.

Minority opinion. Admits to the technical perfection and stylistic refinement of *Rashomon*, but doesn't consider it "immortal art." Calls film decadent and questions its sincerity and forced conclusion. Criticizes the lack of psychological complexity and true critical vision of the world. Does praise the use of imagery to convey dramatic meaning and sound.

368 Griffith, Richard. "*Rashomon*," in *Focus on Rashomon*. Edited by Donald S. Richie. Englewood Cliffs, New Jersey: Prentice-Hall, pp. 35-37. First published in *The Saturday Reivew*, 1952.

369 Harrington, Curtis. "*Rashomon* and the Japanese Cinema," trans. by Elliott Stein in *Focus on Rashomon*. Edited by Donald S. Richie. Englewood Cliffs, New Jersey: Prentice-Hall, pp. 60-65. First published in *Cahiers du cinéma*, 1952.

370 Iwasaki, Akira. "Kurosawa and His Work," in *Focus on Rashomon*. Edited by Donald S. Richie. Englewood Cliffs, N.J.: Prentice-Hall, pp. 21-31. First published in *Japan Quarterly*, 1965.

371 Jacchia, Paolo. "Drama and Lesson of the Defeated," trans. and abridged by Robert M. Connolly, in *Focus on Rashomon*. Edited by Donald S. Richie. Englewood Cliffs, N.J.: Prentice-Hall, pp. 57-60. First published in *Bianco e Nero*, 12, no. 10, October, 1951.

Sees *Rashomon* as a reflection of social, spiritual and human condition. Treats film as a parable. Discusses question of degenerated traditions and collective exigencies.

372 Kaminsky, Stuart M. "The Samurai Film and the Western." *The Journal of Popular Film*, 1, no. 4 (Fall), 312-324.

Comparison of samurai films and Hollywood Westerns. Contrasts *Yojimbo* with *Bad Day at Black Rock* and treats the two versions of *The Magnificent Seven*.

373 McCarten, John. "*Rashomon*," in Focus on *Rashomon*. Edited by Donald S. Richie. Englewood Cliffs, N.J.: Prentice-Hall, pp. 48-49. First published in *The New Yorker*, 1951.

374 Matsue, Yoichi, Kei Kumai, Tadao Sato, Yoshio Shirai, and Koji Yamada. "*Dodeskaden* Spectrum: Akira Kurosawa." Trans. by Haruji Nakamura and Leonard Schrader. *Cinema* [Los Angeles], 7, no. 2 (Spring), 14-17. Reprinted from *Kinema Jumpo*, no. 532, 1970.

Interviews devoted to *Dodeskaden*. Deals with comic elements in the film and the use of comedians as main characters. Talks about working habits during filming and Kurosawa's use of color.

375 Mekas, Jonas. "*Drunken Angel*," in *Movie Journal: The Rise of the New American Cinema, 1959-1971*. New York: Collier Books, pp. 9-10. First published in *The Village Voice*, 1960.

376 Mellen, Joan. "*Dodeskaden:* A Renewal." *Cinema* [Los Angeles], 7, no. 2 (Spring), 20-22.
Notes symbolic meaning of the title. Discusses the conflict between reality and fantasy in the film. Compares film with Kurosawa's *The Lower Depths.* Emphasizes the theme of social deprivation.

377 ———. "The Epic Cinema of Kurosawa." *Take One,* 3, no. 4 (June), 16-19.
Discusses use of the epic genre in the newest art form — film. Talks of emphasis on moral commitment. Compares Kurosawa with Buñuel and Brecht. Notes failure of the hero to change society. Shows how Kurosawa's hero always acts alone and sacrifices for others. Reveals how society is in the process of change and detects the irreconcilability of the classes.

378 Mercier, Pierre. "*Rashomon,* trans. by Elliott Stein in *Focus on Rashomon.* Edited by Donald S. Richie. Englewood Cliffs, N.J.: Prentice-Hall, pp. 49-53. First published in *Cahiers du cinéma,* 1953.

379 Ogi, Masahiro. "Kurosawa, *Dodeskaden* and Japanese Culture." *Cinema* [Los Angeles], 7, no. 2 (Spring), 18-19. First published in *Kinema Jumpo,* 1970.
Comparison of Kurosawa's *Dodeskaden* and *The Lower Depths.* Discusses the long takes and the portrayal of characters.

380 Richie, Donald S., ed. *Focus on Rashomon.* Englewood Cliffs, N.J.: Prentice-Hall, 185 pp.
Critical articles on Kurosawa, his work, and *Rashomon.* Eight contemporary reviews, three contemporary commentaries, and six longer essays. Includes plot synopsis, content outline, script extract, the two short stories by Ryunosuke Akutagawa, filmography with credits, and a selective bibliography. Major contributors include: Donald Richie, R.B. Gadi, Akira Iwasaki, Tadao Sato, Nino Ghelli, Vernon Young, James F. Davidson, and Parker Tyler.

381 Richie, Donald. "*Rashomon,*" in *Focus on Rashomon.* Edited by Donald S. Richie. Englewood Cliffs, N.J.: Prentice-Hall, pp. 71-94. First published in *The Films of Akira Kurosawa,* 1970.
Background information on source material, plot summary, production information, and critical analysis.

382 Sadoul, Georges. "Kurosawa, Akira," in *Dictionary of Film Makers.* Trans., edited and updated by Peter Morris. Berkeley: University of California Press, p. 144.
Brief critical opinion of the director's work, plus a filmography.

383 Sato, Tadao. "*Rashomon,*" trans. by Goro Sato, in *Focus on Rashomon.* Edited by Donald S. Richie. Englewood Cliffs, N.J.: Prentice-Hall, pp. 95-102. First published in *Kurosawa Akira no Sekka,* 1968.
Takes issue with the tendency to interpret *Rashomon* cynically. Sees film as an affirmation of human worth and man's ability to discover objective truth. Calls the work a masterpiece because of "how" it was made. Includes an excerpt of the bandit's attack on the wife. Deals with specific film images.

384 Smith, John M. and Tim Cawkwell, eds. "Kurosawa, Akira," in *The World Encyclopedia of the Film*. New York: World Publishing, 1972, p. 151.
Biographical information and complete filmography up to *Dodeskaden* (1970).

385 T.[ailleur], R.[oger]. "*Akahige (Barberousse)*, de Akira Kurosawa (Japon)." *Positif*, no. 72 (December-January), pp. 9-10.
Positive review. Praises Kurosawa's attention to the underprivileged and his respect for human dignity. Calls work "sublime," "a brilliant study of human nature and feelings."

386 Tessier, Max. "Cinq japonais en quete de films: Akira Kurosawa." *Ecran*, 3, (March), 19-24.
Kurosawa discusses his inactivity since 1965.

387 Tyler, Parker. "*Rashomon* as Modern Art," in *Focus on Rashomon*. Edited by Donald S. Richie. Englewood Cliffs, N.J.: Prentice-Hall, pp. 129-139. First published in *Cinema 16*, pamphlet one, 1952.

388 Young, Vernon. "The Japanese Film: Inquiries and Inferences," in *Focus on Rashomon*. Edited by Donald S. Richie. Englewood Cliffs, N.J.: Prentice-Hall, pp. 110-118. First published in *The Hudson Review*, 1955.

389 _____. "The Japanese Film: Inquires and Inferences and *The Hidden Fortress*: Kurosawa's Comic Mode," in *Vernon Young on Film: Unpopular Essays on a Popular Art*. New York: Quadrangle/The New York Times Book Co., pp. 51-58 and 115-121. First published in *The Hudson Review*, 1955.

390 Zunser, Jesse. "*Rashomon*," in *Focus on Rashomon*. Edited by Donald S. Richie. Englewood Cliffs, N.J.: Prentice-Hall, pp. 37-38. First published in *Cue*, 1951.

1973

391 Anderson, J.[oseph] L. "Japanese Swordfighters and American Gunfighters." *Cinema Journal*, 12, no. 2 (Spring), 1-21.
Deals with traditions and background of the samurai films with brief mention of *Yojimbo* and *Sanjuro*.

392 Beylie, Claude. "*L'idiot*." *Ecran*, no. 14 (April), pp. 62-63.
Discusses Kurosawa's veneration for the text. Feels work a triumph alongside Murnau's *Faust* and Dreyer's *Gertrud*. Comments on the theme — the ruin of a pure man — and background information on distribution problems.

*393 Chevallier, Jacques. "*L'idiot*." *Revue du cinéma*, no. 272, (May), pp. 105-107.
Cited in *Film Literature Index*, vol. 1, Albany, N.Y.: Filmdex, 1973, p. 173.

394 Erens, Patricia. "*Throne of Blood* and *Macbeth*." Program Notes. Chicago: The Film Center, School of The Art Institute (7, 14 September).

Comparison of Kurosawa's *The Throne of Blood* and Orson Welles' *Macbeth*. Concentrates on the originality and technical and artistic innovations of the two.

395   Gerlach, John. "Shakespeare, Kurosawa and *Macbeth*: A Response to J. Blumenthal." *Literature/Film Quarterly*, 1, no. 4 (Fall), 352-359.

Expresses disappointment with Kurosawa's adaptation. Deals with his use of duration. Discusses lack of access to Washizu's inner feelings and Kurosawa's efforts to make him more acceptable. Claims Kurosawa upsets the balance of "sympathy for and judgment against Macbeth."

396   *Kurosawa Retrospective.* Program Schedule. Philadelphia: TLA Cinema (Fall).

Contains information on twenty-five Kurosawa films, a biography, critique, and an analysis of the director's style.

397   Linden, George W. "Five Views of Rashomon." *Soundings*, 56 (Winter), 393-411.

Analyzes *Rashomon* as a commercial venture, as a work of art, as a cultural allegory, as a film, and as a philosophic statement, especially a rendering of Buddhist psychology/metaphysics.

*398   Mesnil, Michel. *Kurosawa.* Paris: Seghers, 171 pp.

A critical work on the films of Kurosawa. Includes a filmography and bibliography. Cited in *National Union Catalog*, vol. 11. Washington: Library of Congress, 1974, p. 337.

399   Mullin, Michael, "Macbeth on Film." *Literature/Film Quarterly*, 1, no. 4 (Fall), 332-342.

Compares four versions of *Macbeth* — Kurosawa's, Orson Welles', George Schaefer's, and Roman Polanski's. Agrees with former critics that *The Throne of Blood* is one of the best adaptations of Shakespeare to the screen. Sees other versions as flawed. Cites the need to consider more than "textual accuracy." Treats realistic and naturalistic aspects of the film on several levels.

400   N.[iogret], H.[ubert]. "L'idiot." *Positif*, no. 150 (May), pp. 84-85.

Favorable review. Feels Kurosawa succeeds in painting Dostoyevsky's inner drama in a three hour film which never abates in tension.

401   Passek, Jean-Loup. "L'idiot." *Cinema '73*, no. 174 (March), pp. 127-128.

Favorable review. Claims the film "shines with a thousand fires and is indisputably evident as the best adaptation ever filmed of a Dostoyevsky novel," despite the deletion of one hour by the Shochiku Company. Cites faults, however, including a theatrical construction, uneven interpretation, and weak performance by Mifune.

402   Tucker, Richard N. "Kurosawa and Ichikawa: feudalist and individualist," in *Japan: Film Image.* London: Studio Vista, pp. 74-84.

Book divides directors into the ethical left and ethical right. Treats the importance of social context in Kurosawa's work. Comments on Kurosawa's style, camera techniques, and narrative constructions. Differs with Richie on question of feudal elements in Kurosawa's films. Sees central characters as limited individuals.

403 Weinberg, Herman G. "Coffee, Brandy and Cigars," in *Saint Cinema; Writings on Film 1929-1970*. New York: Dover Publications, p. 257. First published in *Variety*, 1966.
   Brief mention of the effect of *Dodeskaden's* commercial failure on Kurosawa's life.

1974

*404 Anon. "Dodes'Da-den." *Independent Film Journal* 13 November).
   Cited in Aceto, Vincent J., Jane Graves and Fred Silva, eds. *Film Literature Index*, vol. 2. Albany, N.Y.: Filmdex, 1974, p. 140.

405 Anon. "Slow-Going Upbuild of Foreign Film Directors in U.S. — Per Kurosawa." *Variety* (18 December).
   Deals with Kurosawa's increasing reputation in U.S. Compares director with Ingmar Bergman.

406 Almendarez, Valentin. "*Rashomon.*" *Cinema Texas* (Austin: University of Texas), 6, no. 30 (19 March), 1-5.
   Background on the Japanese cinema. Treats the questions of existentialism in the film. Includes quotations from several critics.

407 Barrot, Olivier. "Dodes'caden." *Ecran*, no. 31 (December), p. 77.
   Refers to film as a "song of disconsolate love" for mankind. Discusses how Kurosawa meticulously paints the "lower depths" in an allegorical manner, depicting conditions of life within a modern town and its effect upon its inhabitants.

*408 Bassam, Raphael. "Dodes'caden." *Telecine*, no. 194 (December), p. 22.
   Cited in Aceto, Vincent J., Jane Graves and Fred Silva, eds. *Film Literature Index*, vol. 2, Albany, N.Y.: Filmdex, 1974, p. 140.

409 Blumenthal, J[erry]. "*Macbeth* into *Throne of Blood*," in *Film Theory and Criticism: Introductory Readings*. Edited by Gerald Mast and Marshall Cohen. New York: Oxford University Press, pp. 340-351. Reprinted from *Sight and Sound*, 1965.

410 "The Films of Akira Kurosawa: A Retrospective." Program Notes. Berkeley, Calif.: Pacific Film Archives, University Art Museum (5 January), 4 pp.
   Notes on Kurosawa's career and twenty films (*Sanshiro Sugata* to *Dodeskaden*) adapted from Donald Richie's book.

411 Kael, Pauline. "*Yojimbo*," in *Film Theory and Criticism*. New York: Oxford University Press, pp. 417-421. First published in *The Partisan Review*, 1963.

412 Kaminsky, Stuart M. "Comparative Forms: The Samurai Film and the Western," in *American Film Genres*. Dayton, Ohio: Pflaum Publishing, pp. 33-42. Reprinted by Dell Publishing Co., 1977. First published by *The Journal of Popular Film*, 1972.

413 Kauffmann, Stanley. "*Rashomon.*" *Horizon*, 16, no. 2 (Spring), 36-43. Reprinted in *Living Images*, 1975.

Gives background and plot. Questions why the film made such an impact. Notes Western influences on Kurosawa. Discusses the film's accessibility, the acting, the blocks of visual texture, and the quality of motion in the forest scenes. Claims film shows the truth of the ego as a motivating force in life, a universal phenomenon. Well illustrated.

414 Kurosawa, Akira, Yoichi Matsue, Tamotsu Kawasaki, Teruyo Nogami, Asakazu Nakai, Norio Minoshima, Takamaro Shimaji, and Yoshio Shirai. "Kurosawa Akira Kantoku to *Dersu Uzala* Staff ni Kiku" [Listening to Kurosawa and His Staff of *Dersu Uzala*]. *Kinema Jumpo* (first issue October), pp. 112-121.

Kurosawa discusses the difficulties of working with Russian actors and crew and his efforts to capture nature on film, which he names as the real hero of *Dersu Uzala*. The director calls for financial help from the Japanese government to help young people make films and bemoans the fact that no successor has yet appeared to replace him.

415 Milne, Tom. "*Hakuchi (The Idiot).*" *Monthly Film Bulletin*, 41 (March), 41.

Sees the film as an essential rendering of the spirit of Dostoyevsky's novel. Concentrates on Kurosawa's triangular compositions. Despite previous bad press, feels the film is "strange," "poetic," and one of Kurosawa's best films. Includes a plot summary and credits.

416 Noureddine, Ghali. "Sur les ecrans." *Juene Cinema*, no. 83 (December-January), pp. 34-36.

Discusses the commercial failure of *Dodeskaden* and its effect on Kurosawa's life. Treats Kuroswa's presentation of "the little people" as adapted to contemporary times and his portrayal of human misery. Calls film "tender and heart-rending," "a film lament."

417 Passek, Jean-Loup. "*Dodes'caden.*" *Cinema '74*, no. 193 (December), pp. 108-110.

Discusses the film's psychological closeness to *Ikiru* and *The Idiot*, especially in its description of "marginal humanity" and the "Prince Muychkine character" who possesses the virtue of goodness. Talks about the theatrical space and fantastic color. Includes brief plot summary.

418 Robinson, Davis. *The History of World Cinema*. New York: Stein and Day, pp. 272-274.

Refers to Kurosawa as the most gifted director of the immediate postwar period.

419 Shimaji, Takamaro, ed. *Kinema Jumpo*, Special Issue on Akira Kurosawa, no. 631 (7 May), 274 pp.

Contains complete screenplay for *Dersu Uzala* and an article by Kurosawa naming the film as the completion of a thirty-year old dream. Comments by Yoichi Matsue, producer of *Dersu Uzala*. Section with testimonies to Kurosawa's creativity by actors and many crew members. Last part contains reference material on Kurosawa's work.

420 Wolf, Barbara. "On Akira Kurosawa." *The Yale Review*, 64, no. 2, pp. 218-226.
Cites the undistinguished nature of Kurosawa's material. Sees the main theme of his films as the impossibility of escaping the human condition. Calls the films a blend of realism and allegory. Notes the difference etween characters who speak for themselves and the complete works which speak for Kurosawa. Draws examples from *Seven Samurai* and compares with Shakespeare's *Hamlet*.

421 Zambrano, Ana Laura. "*Throne of Blood*: Kurosawa's *Macbeth*." *Literature/Film Quarterly*, 2, no. 3 (Summer), 262-274.
Shows how Kurosawa recasts Shakespeare's *Macbeth* into a totally Japanese form drawing on elements from medieval picture scrolls, Buddhist sculpture, Japanese mythology, traditional literature, and Noh drama. Deals with various themes including the family, society, the cyclical and transitory nature of life, and the question of evil and passion. Also discusses Japanese aesthetic traditions which seek to redefine, not imitate reality.

422 No entry.

1975

423 Anon. "*Dodeskaden*." *Avant-Scene*, no. 155 (February), pp. 42-45.
Plot summary. Quotations by Kurosawa and critical comments from the French press.

424 Anon. "Kurosawa Workshops I-IV." Program Notes. University of Calgary (25 January, 1 February, 8 February, and 15 February).
Contains background material on Kurosawa, the actors, and the following films: *The Throne of Blood, Yojimbo, Seven Samurai*, and *Record of a Living Being*.

425 Anon. "Movies." *Soviet Life Magazine*, 12 (December), p. 62.
A note on *Dersu Uzala* and its award in Moscow.

426 Barr, Alan P. "Exquisite Comedy and The Dimensions of Heroism: Akira Kurosawa's *Yojimbo*." *The Massachusetts Review*, 16, no. 1, pp. 158-168.
Comparison of *Yojimbo* and *High Noon*. Treats the questions of setting, allegory, and Christian metaphor. Deals with the comic elements of *Yojimbo* and Kurosawa's reworking of the concept of the hero. Shows how characters' physical traits reflect his inner nature.

*427 Bazin, Andre. *Le cinéma de la cruauté*. Paris: Flammarion, 224 pp.
Includes section on the work of Kurosawa. Cited in *National Union Catalog*, vol. 2. Washington: Library of Congress, 1977, p. 90.

428 Bohn, Thomas W. and Richard L. Stromgren. "Kurosawa and Ray," in *Light and Shadows: A History of Motion Pictures*. Port Washington, N.Y.: Alfred Publishing Co., pp. 374-377.

Discusses the importance of *Rashomon* in establishing Kurosawa as an international director and in turning attention to the Japanese cinema.

*429 Estève, Michel. "Cinema estranger." *Cinématographe*, no. 11 (January-February), pp. 12-24.

Cited in Aceto, Vincent J., Jane Graves, and Fred Silva, eds. *Film Literature Index*, vol. 3, 1975, p. 320.

430 Demby, Betty Jeffries. "Moscow Film Festival." *Filmmakers Newsletter*, 8, no. 12 (12 October), 65-70.

Plot summary of *Dersu Uzala*. Comments on the production by Kurosawa.

431 Giles, Dennis. "Kurosawa's Heroes." *Arion* (NS), 2, no. 2, pp. 270-299.

Defines the hero as a person who stands apart from the rest of the world; who knows that death is the goal of life and therefore can risk dying. Sees villains as representatives of the status quo. Heroes break the circle. Long section on the process of awakening in *Ikiru*. Also comments on the failed heroes of *The Bad Sleep Well* and *I Live in Fear*. Treats mythic elements in *Yojimbo* and provides a defense for *The Quiet Duel*.

432 Gliserman, Marty. "*Dodes'Ka-Den*: Illusions." *Jump Cut*, no. 6 (March-April), p. 1.

Criticism of the film on ideological grounds. Claims that Kurosawa has romanticized the urban poor and ignored oppression by a veneer of aesthetics. Feels that Kurosawa's theme suggests the way to avoid unbearable realities is through dreams and fantasies.

433 Kauffmann, Stanley. "*Rashomon*," in *Living Images; Film Comment and Criticism*. New York: Harper and Row, pp. 316-324. First published in *Horizon*, 1974.

434 Mellen, Joan. "Akira Kurosawa," in *Voices From the Japanese Cinema*. New York: Liveright, pp. 37-58.

Interview with Kurosawa. Mellen refers to him as the "sole living master" and a director who transcends all easy categories." Discusses how he raised the jidai-geki to an art form. Includes comments by leading Japanese critics. Kurosawa discusses early political commitments and often contradicts Mellen's interpretations.

435 Robinson, David. "*Dodeskaden*." *Monthly Film Bulletin*, 42 (May), 103.

Compares the film to Kurosawa's *The Lower Depths*. Notes cut from 224 to 100 minutes. Discusses the use of color, creation of caricatures, and the acting style.

436 Silver, Alain. "Samurai." *Film Comment*, 11, no. 5 (September-October), 10-15.

Comments on *Yojimbo*, *Seven Samurai*, and *Sanjuro* in relation to other postwar samurai films, especially in terms of narrative and character conventions.

437 Simone, R. Thomas. "The Mythos of 'The Sickness Unto Death': Kurosawa's *Ikiru* and Tolstoy's *The Death of Ivan Ilych*." *Literature/Film Quarterly*, 3, no. 1 (Winter), 2-12.

Discusses Kierkegaard's concept of spiritual disease of despair and death as it manifests itself in Kurosawa's *Ikiru* and Tolstoy's *The Death of Ivan Ilych*. Compares Tolstoy's solitary vision with Kurosawa's commitment to communal action. Treats differences between literary and cinematic forms.

438   Sineaux, Michel. "Éloge de la folie." *Positif*, no. 165 (January), pp. 10-11.

Analysis of *Dodeskaden* as the convergence of three genres previously treated separately: contemporary realism as in *Ikiru*, neo-realistic melodrama as in *One Wonderful Sunday*, and metaphysical drama as in his adaptations of Western writers. Cites Kurosawa's choice of a short shooting schedule, the use of television actors, and his experimentation with color.

439   Tessier, Max. "Tovaritch Kurosawa." *Ecran*, no. 33 (February), pp. 3-4.

Discusses the details of inception, cost, production, casting, filming and distribution of *Dersu Uzala*. Claims that Kurosawa's future rests on the success of the film.

440   Turell, Saul J. and Jeff Lieberman. "Music and Sound" [*Dodeskaden*] and "The Director [*Rashomon and Dodeskaden*], in *The Art of Film*. Chicago: Perspective Films, pp. 42, 70-71.

Deals with use of subjective sound in opening of *Dodeskaden* and comments on Kurosawa as a director.

441   Werb. "*Dersu Uzala.*" *Variety* (13 August), p. 16.

Calls the film "heartwarming" and the subject one of "human uplift." Recommends tightening work for Western audiences. Includes plot summary.

1976

442   Anon. "Cinema." *Time*, 108, no. 17 (25 October), 80.

Favorable review of *Dersu Uzala*. Refers to its "moments of real majesty" and "the clear resonance of genius." Plot summary.

443   Anon. "Kurosawa Tenno Desae" [Even 'Emperor' Kurosawa...]. *The Nikkan Sports* (26 May), p. 15.

Discusses problems of Japanese directors, even those of stature, to raise money for new projects. Notes pressure exerted on older directors to train younger men instead of making movies. Discusses Kurosawa's inability to gain approval from Toho to film *Midare* [*Corruption*] based on Shakespeare's *King Lear*. States wish of many that Kurosawa's *Dersu Uzala* had been made in Japan.

444   Anon. "Pictures at an Exhibition." *Newsweek*, 88 (18 October), 115.

Short note on *Dersu Uzala*. Refers to the film's "awesome filming of nature."

445   Armes, Roy. *The Ambiguous Image*. Bloomington: Indiana University Press, pp. 25-26.

Cites *Rashomon* as a forerunner of the modernist cinema because of its ambiguity and unresolved enigmas.

446   Eder, Richard. "Contrasts Evident in Japanese-Soviet Movie." *The New York Times* (5 October), p. 54.

116 / AKIRA KUROSAWA

Review of *Dersu Uzala*. Calls the first half "delicate and haunting" and the second half "numb and ponderous." Plot summary.

447 Guild, Hazel. "Kurosawa Slaps Soviets For Cutting Jointly-Made film." *Variety* (17 November), p. 1.
Treats argument over the cut version of *Dersu Uzala* made for Italian distribution. Cites Kurosawa's anger about the twenty minute deletion made without his consent.

448 Imaizumi, Yukiko. "Notes on Kurosawa." *The Thousand Eyes Magazine*, no. 9 (April), p. 7.
Background on Kurosawa from 1965 to 1970. Main emphasis on reception of *Dersu Uzala*.

449 Leyda, Jay. "Historical Perspectives: The Films of Kurosawa." *The Thousand Eyes Magazine*, no. 8 (March), pp. 5-6. First published in *Sight and Sound*, 1954.
Additional credits for *Rashomon*.

450 Mellen, Joan. *The Waves at Genji's Door: Japan Through Its Cinema*. New York: Pantheon Books, pp. 22-26, 41-56, 202-206, 229-235, 407-412 and passim.
Critical analysis of Kurosawa's major films with emphasis on political implications, portrayal of women, cultural priorities, and socio-historical background. Notes how films reflect the postwar realities and psychological mood of Japan. Discusses the degree to which Kurosawa accepts or revolts against the feudal standards of Japanese society.

450a Rhode, Eric. *A History of the Cinema From Its Origins to 1970*. New York: Hill and Wang, pp. 490-493, 513-514 and 519-523.
Discusses the importance and impact of *Rashomon* on the Japanese cinema. Refers to Kurosawa as a 'neo-realist' director who sees man as either a wild beast or a fallen angel. Criticizes his naïveté and sense of humor, although he has high regard for Kurosawa's editing style. Offers a political interpretation for several films, including *Rashomon* and *Seven Samurai*, the latter which he views as reactionary in nature. A rather offbeat, unflattering assessment of Kurosawa's work.

451 Richie, Donald. "Kurosawa: A Television Script." *The Thousand Eyes Magazine*, no. 10 (May), pp. 3-5.
Published script for 1½ hour documentary film on Kurosawa shown in Japan in June, 1975, written by Richie. Film includes general comments on major themes and style with representative film clips and interviews with actors from Kurosawa's repertory group.

452 Seaman, Ann Rowe. "The Lower Depths." *Cinema Texas* (Austin: University of Texas), 10, no. 4 (28 April), 67-74.
General comments on the Japanese film industry and the jidai-geki. Includes a plot summary, information on Gorky, background on Buddhism and character analysis, especially of Kahei. Includes a reading list.

453 _____. "Sanjuro." *Cinema Texas* (Austin: University of Texas), 10, no. 4 (5 May), pp. 99-105.

Discusses the film in relation to the American Western and as a genre film. Treats the topic of political corruption and illusion vs. reality. Includes a plot summary and a reading list.

1977

454 Daney, Serge. "Un our en plus (*Dersu Uzala*)." *Cahiers du cinéma*, no. 274 (March), pp. 33-40.

Discusses the film in terms of the fictive space delineated by the camera and illustrated by the characters. Contrasts the geographer Dersu, who sees broadly with the soldier Arseniev, who sees accurately. Points out Arseniev's narrow range of vision. Talks of the imaginary space between the two men which holds them together and how the camera registers the contradictions in their perceptions.

455 Jorgens, Jack J. "Defining *Macbeth*: Schaefer, Welles, and Kurosawa," in *Shakespeare on Film*. Bloomington: Indiana University Press, pp. 148-160.

Comparison of Kurosawa's version with those of George Schaefer and Orson Welles. Sees *The Throne of Blood* as a tragedy of Fate, man caught between the moral order which he created and an impersonal natural order embodied by the Forest Spirit. Notes the sense of entrapment. Characterizes film as a conflict between the forest and the fortress.

456 Kurtz, Patricia. "Akira Kurosawa." *Single Take*, 1, no. 1 (Spring), 49-55.

Deals with Kurosawa's life and career. Emphasis on the search for moral purpose and belief in symbolic regeneration in his work. Discussion of the degree to which his films reflect a Japanese perspective.

457 McCormick, Ruth. "Kurosawa: The Nature of Heroism." *The Thousand Eyes Magazine* (April), pp. 8-9.

Notes Kurosawa's recent neglect here and in Japan. Defines Kurosawa's hero as one who must make a choice. Sees films as increasingly pessimistic.

458 Silver, Alain. "Akira Kurosawa," in *The Samurai Film*. Cranbury, N.J.: A.S. Barnes, pp. 43-53.

Discusses the visual aspects and pictorialism of *The Throne of Blood, Rashomon, and Seven Samurai*. Treats *Yojimbo* and *Sanjuro* in terms of genre typing.

No Date

459 Anon. "Interview with Akira Kurosawa," in *Kurosawa*. Program Booklet. Uppsala: Uppsala Studenters Filmstudio, pp. 25-28. First published in *Cinema*, 1963.

460 Anon. *Kurosawa*. Program Booklet. Uppsala: Uppsala Studenters Filmstudio. 51 pp.

Contains a reprint of an interview with Kurosawa in Swedish as well as reprints in English of the following articles: "Kurosawa" by Shinbi Iida, "Interview with Akira Kurosawa" by *Cinema*, and "Kurosawa on Kurosawa" by Donald Richie.

461 Anon. "*Les sept samourais.*" *Les lettres francaises*, no. 597.
Deals with the film as genre work, another "tendency" film like those which appeared before and after the War.

462 Anon. "*Rashomon.*" *Les lettres francaises*, no. 354.
Review of the film as an indicator of a postwar Japanese attitudes, especially concerning the unwillingness to accept social responsibility.

*463 Anon. "Regards sur le cinéma japonais." *Revue internationale du cinéma*, no. 14.
Cited in Richie (269), p. 212.

*464 El-Bahi, Abdeljelil. "*Rashomon.*" *I.D.H.E.C.* [Paris], no. 145.
Cited in Richie (269), p. 214.

465 Iida, Shinbi. "Kurosawa," in *Kurosawa*. Program Booklet. Uppsala; Uppsala Studenters Filmstudio, pp. 20-24. First published in *Cinema*, 1963.

*465a *Kurosawa Akira* [Akira Kurosawa]. Tokyo: Toho Publications Section.
Detailed information on Kurosawa's work by the filmmaker. Cited in Richie (269), p. 213.

466 Richie, Donald. "Kurosawa on Kurosawa," in *Kurosawa. Program Booklet. Uppsala: Uppsala Studenters Filmstudio, pp. 29-44. First published in Sight and Sound, 1964.*

467 Seton, Marie. "Akira Kurosawa: des classiques russes et anglais pour fair réfléchir les japonais." *Radio-cinéma-télévision*, no. 417.
Interview in which Kurosawa speaks of his preference for Russian literary sources over Japanese works because of their focus on character motivation. Discusses his concentration on male characters. Feels that due to tradition, Japanese women have less to express. Comments on the fact that the Japanese have lost contact with their own culture.

*468 Vvoire (d'), Jean. "Les sept samourais." *Telerama*, no. 679.
Cited in Richie (269), p. 214.

*469 Zendel, Jose. "*Rashomon.*" *Les lettres francaises*, no. 411.
Cited in Richie (269), p. 214.

Performances and Writings

FILM APPEARANCES

470   1975 *Akira Kurosawa: Film Director*
      d: Donald Richie

WRITINGS

1941

471   *Daruma-dera no Doitsujin* [*A German at the Daruma Temple*].
      Published in *Eiga Hyoron* magazine.

472   *Uma* [*Horses*]. Co-scripted with Kajiro Yamamoto.
      Tells of a young girl's care and affection for a colt which eventually is taken from her by the army. Directed by Kajiro Yamamoto.

1942

473   *Seishun no Kiryu* [*Currents of Youth*].
      Directed by Osamu Fuchimizu.

474   *Shizukanari* [*All is Quiet*].
      Published in *Nihon Eiga* magazine.

475   *Tsubasa no Gaika* [*A Triumph of Wings*].
      Directed by Satsuo Yamamoto.

1944

476   *Dohyo-matsuri* [*Wrestling-Ring Festival*].
      Directed by Santaro Marune.

1945

477   *Appare Isshin Tasuke* [*Bravo, Tasuke Isshin!*].
      Directed by Kiyoshi Saeki.

1947

478 *Ginrei no Hate* [*To the End of the Silver Mountains*].
Co-scripted with Kajiro Yamamoto. Directed by Senkichi Taniguchi.

479 *Hatsukoi* [*First Love*].
Section of *Yottsu no Koi no Monogatari* [*Four Love Stories*]. Directed by Shiro Toyoda.

480 *Yuki (Snow)*.

1948

481 *Shozo* [*The Portrait*]
Directed by Keisuke Kinoshita.

1949

482 *Jakoman to Tetsu* [*Jakoman and Tetsu*].
Depicts the rough frontier life in an Hokkaido fishing village. Directed by Senkichi Taniguchi.

483 *Jigoku no Kifujin* [*The Lady from Hell*].
Dramatizes political corruption, black marketeering and the decline of the nobility. Directed by Yotoyoshi Oda.

1950

484 *Akatsuki no Dasso* [*Escape at Dawn*].
Story of army cruelty portrayed through a soldier's desertion and his love for a "consolation girl" in China. His comrades are ordered to shoot him. They refuse, but the commanding officer kills him as he attempts to flee. Directed by Senkichi Taniguchi.

485 *Jiruba no Tetsu* [*Tetsu 'Jilba'*].
Directed by Isamu Kosugi.

486 *Tateshi Danpei* [*Fencing Master*].
Directed by Masahiro Makino.

1951

487 *Ai to Nikushimi no Kanata e* [*Beyond Love and Hate*].
Tells of a prisoner who, believing his wife has been unfaithful, escapes and hides in a remote mountain. He defends himself with a rifle, but is eventually captured. Directed by Senkichi Taniguchi.

488 *Kedamono no Yado* [*The Den of Beasts*].
Directed by Tatsuo Osone.

489 *Ketto Kagiya no Tsuji* [*The Duel at Kagiya Corner*].
Directed by Issei Mori.

1955

490 *Sugata Sanshiro* [*Sanshiro Sugata*].
Remade under its original title directed by Shigeo Tanaka.

1957

491 *Tekichu Odan Sanbyakuri* [*Three Hundred Miles through Enemy Lines*].
Directed by Issei Mori.

1960

492 *Sengoku Guntoden* [*The Saga of the Vagabond*].
Directed by Toshio Sugie.

1961

493 *The Magnificent Seven.*
Remake of *Seven Samurai*. Directed by John Sturges.

1964

494 *The Outrage.*
Remake of *Rashomon*. Directed by Martin Ritt.

495 *Per un pungo di dollari* [*A Fistful of Dollars*].
Remake of *Yojimbo*. Directed by Sergio Leoni.

1965

496 *Sugata Sanshiro* [*Sanshiro Sugata*].
Remade under original title. Directed by Seiichiro Uchikawa. Edited by Kurosawa.

1976

497 *Ran* [Chaos]. Adaptation of *King Lear*. Unpublished.

1977-1978

498 *The Masque of Black Death* (No Japanese title). Adaptation from Edgar Allan Poe. Unpublished.

No Date

499 *Dokkoi kono Yari* [*The Lifted Spear*].

500 *Jajauma Monogatari* [*The Story of the Shrew*].

501 *Mori no Senichiya* [*A Thousand and One Nights in the Forest*].

Archival Sources

AUSTRIA

502 Oesterreichisches Filmmuseum
Augustinerstrasse 1,
1010 Wein (Vienna)
tel: 52 34 26, 52 62 06
- *High and Low*
- *The Most Beautiful*
- *No Regrets For Our Youth*
- *One Wonderful Sunday*
- *Rashomon*
- *Sanshiro Sugata*
- *Seven Samurai*
- *Stray Dog*
- *Those Who Make Tomorrow*
- *The Throne of Blood*
- Director Kurosawa (by Donald Richie in Japanese, no subtitles).

Available only on premises.

CANADA

503 National Film Archives
395 Wellington
Ottawa K1A ON3
tel: 995-1311
- *Rashomon*
- *Sanjuro*

Available only on premises.

DENMARK

504 The Danish Film Museum
St. Sondervoldstraede
1419 Kobenhavn K.
ASTA 6500

The Hidden Fortress
Rashomon
Yojimbo
Available only on premises.

FRANCE

505 Centre National de la Cinematographie
Archives Du Film
78390 Bois D'Arcy
tel: 460-20-50
The Hidden Fortress
Ikiru
Rashomon
Seven Samurai

INDIA

506 National Film Archive of India
Law College Road
Poona 411004
tel: 58516
The Hidden Fortress
Ikiru
The Lower Depths
Rashomon
Red Beard
Sanshiro Sugata
Seven Samurai
The Throne of Blood
Available only on premises.

ITALY

507 Cineteca Nazionale
Presso Il Centro Sperimentale Di Cinematografia
Via Tuscolana N. 1524
00173 Roma
tel: 740046
The Hidden Fortress
Seven Samurai
The Throne of Blood

JAPAN

508 National Film Center
2-11 Kyobashi
Chuo-ku, Tokyo
Archive holds a print of all Kurosawa films.

SWEDEN

509 Swedish Film Institute
Filmhuset
Box 27 126
102 52 Stockholm 27
> *Dodeskaden*
> *Drunken Angel*
> *The Hidden Fortress*
> *The Idiot*
> *The Lower Depths*
> *The Men Who Tread on the Tiger's Tail*
> *Rashomon*
> *Yojimbo*

UNITED STATES OF AMERICA

510 Library of Congress
Motion Picture Section
Washington, D.C. 20540
> *Ikiru*
> *The Most Beautiful*
> *Sanshiro Sugata*

511 Museum of Modern Art
Department of Film
11 West 53rd Street
New York, N.Y. 10019
> *Seven Samurai*

Film Distributors

(16 mm)

512 Audio Brandon Films (Macmillan)
34 MacQuesten Parkway So.
Mount Vernon, N.Y. 10550
The Bad Sleep Well
Drunken Angel
The Lower Depths
The Men Who Tread on the Tiger's Tail
The Quiet Duel
Record of a Living Being
Red Beard
Sanjuro
Sanshiro Sugata
Scandal
Seven Samurai
Stray Dog
The Throne of Blood
Yojimbo

513 Film Images (A division of Radium Films, Inc.)
17 West 60th Street
New York, N.Y. 10023
The Hidden Fortress

514 Janus Films
745 Fifth Avenue
New York, N.Y. 10022
High and Low

515 New Yorker Films
43 West 61st Street
New York, N.Y. 10023
The Idiot

Author Index

Aida, Kimi 340
Almendarez, Valentin 406
Alpert, Hollis 151, 190
Amengual, Barthélemy 228, 229
Anby 108, 109, 173
Anderson, Joseph L. 52, 92, 97, 110, 152, 391
Anderson, Lindsay 83
Anon. 31-34, 58, 65-68, 81, 82, 96, 104-107, 125-127, 146-150, 174-189, 224-227, 257-259, 286, 298, 303, 357, 358, 404, 405, 423-425, 442-444, 459-463

Barbarow, George 35, 359
Barnes, Peter 59
Barr, Alan P. 426
Barrot, Olivier 407
Bassam, Raphael 408
Bazin, Andre 84, 427
Beaufort, John 36, 360
Beck, James M. 230
Bernhardt, William 111, 153
Beylie, Claude 392
Billard, Pierre 231
Blumenthal, Jerry 260, 315, 316, 409
Bobker, Lee R. 304
Brook, Peter 261
Bucher, Felix 276

Callenbach, Ernest 341
Cavander, Kenneth 93
Chekhonin, B. 317
Chevallier, Jacques 393
Clarens, Carlos 127
Clurman, Harold 342
Cohn, Bernard 343
Cowie, Peter 277
Crawford, Stanley 262
Crist, Judith 191, 299
Crowdus, Gary 344
Crowther, Bosley 27, 37, 69, 98, 112, 128, 154-156, 192, 193, 232, 288, 289, 361, 362

Daney, Serge 454
Davidson, James F. 55, 305, 363
Davis, Richard 306
Demby, Betty Jeffries 430
Dent, Alan 38
Dillingham, Harold 157, 194
Dyer, Peter John 99

Eder, Richard 446
El-Bahi, Abdeljelil 464
Erens, Patricia 394
Estéve, Michel 228, 233-236, 429
Ezratty, Sacha 237, 290

Falk, Ray 39
Farber, Manny 40, 364
Foster, Hugh G. 129
Fox, Charles 94

G., J. 365
Gadi, R. B. 278, 366
Gaffary, F. 85
Gerlach, John 395
Ghelli, Nino 367
Giles, Dennis 431
Gill, Brendan 130, 158, 195, 196, 238
Gillett, John 318, 367
Giuglaris, Marcel 70
Giuglaris, Shinobu 70
Glazer, Nathan 239
Gliserman, Marty 432
Gow, Gordon 131, 319, 345
Greenspun, Roger 346
Griffith, Richard 41, 368
Guild, Hazel 447

H. J. 113
Hall, Peter 307
Handiquet, Philippe 228, 240
Harcourt-Smith, Simon 42
Harrington, Curtis 43, 369

Hart, Henry 44
Hartung, Philip T. 45, 71, 132, 159, 197, 198, 291
Hashimoto, Shinobu 199, 309
Hatch, Robert 72
Hawk 133, 200, 263
Henry, Jim 347
Higham, Charles 264
Hines, T. S. 73
Hirai, Yoshio 241
Holmes, Winifred 100
Hull, David Stewart 160

Iida, Shinbi 201, 465
Iijima, Tadashi 202, 228, 242
Imaizumi, Yukiko 448
Ishii, Kenneth 244
Iwabutchi, Masayoshi 134
Iwasaki, Akira 86, 265, 320, 370

Jacchia, Paolo 371
Jarvie, Ian 245
Jorgens, Jack J. 455

Kael, Pauline 203, 266, 411
Kaminsky, Stuart M. 372, 412
Kass, Robert 46
Kauffmann, Stanley 47, 114, 135, 161, 162, 204-207, 279, 308, 413, 433
Kenny, Don 348-351
Kirby, Gordon 95
Knight, Arthur 74, 87, 115
Kofujida, Chieko 321
Kurosawa, Akira 86, 208, 209, 246, 247, 300, 309, 322, 352, 414
Kurtz, Patricia 456

Labarrere, Andre 228, 248
Lajeunesse, Jacqueline
Langlois, Henri 210
Leirens, Jean 136
Leonard, Harold 75
Leyda, Jay 56, 76, 449
Linden, George W. 397

M., J. 292
McCarten, John 28, 77, 116, 373
McCormick, Ruth 457
MacDonald, Dwight 137, 138, 163, 267, 310
McDonald, Gerald D. 48
McVay, Douglas 139, 140
Manvell, Roger 353
Matsue, Yoichi 323, 374
Mekas, Jonas 117, 118, 164, 165, 211, 375
Mellen, Joan 376, 377, 434, 450
Mercier, Pierre 53, 378
Mesnil, Michel 280, 398

Mifune, Toshiro 249
Mills, William E. 78, 79
Milne, Tom 415
Miner, Earl Roy 80
Mosk 324
Moullet, Luc 89
Mullin, Michael 399
Myro 101, 212

Niogret, Hubert 354, 400
Nogami, Teruyo 326
Noureddine, Ghali 416

Ogi, Masahiro 379
Ortalani, Benito 268

Passek, Jean-Loup 401, 417
Perrin, Claude 228, 250
Pesce, Alberto 228, 251
Pinto, Alfonso 293

Quigly, Isabel 141

Rhode, Eric 450a
Richard, Tony 60
Richie, Donald 110, 119, 120, 142, 143, 166, 167, 213-216, 252, 269, 270, 281, 294, 311, 312, 327, 328, 355, 380, 381, 451, 466, 470, 502
Rieupeyrout, Jean-Louis 61
Robinson, David 418, 435
Roemer, Michael 121
Roman, Robert C. 122
Rosenthal, A. 57

Sadoul, Georges 54, 271, 282
Sarris, Andrew 252a
Sato, Tadao 272, 301, 329, 383
Seaman, Ann Rowe 452, 453
Sesonske, Alexander 295
Seton, Marie 467
Sherwin, Sally 253
Shibata, Hayao 282
Shigeno, Tatsuhiko 49
Shimaji, Takamaro 330, 331, 419
Shimizu, Chiyota 29, 228, 254
Shinoda, Yukichi 333
Shirai, Yoshio 217, 282, 334
S.(how) B.(usiness) I.(llustrated) 168
Silke, James 218-220
Silver, Alain 436, 458
Silverstein, Norman 273
Simone, R. Thomas 437
Sineaux, Michel 438
Smith, John M. 384
Strauss, Harold 62
Strick, Philip 335

Suda, Motoji 90
Sugimura, Haruko 255
Svenson, Arne 356

Tailleur, Roger 274, 385
Takeda, Taijun 256
Tayama, Rikiya 336
Tessier, Max 386, 439
Thirard, Paul-Louis 91
Thomas, John 275
Thompson, Howard, 123, 221, 222, 283, 302
Tokawa, Naoki 210, 337
Torok, Jean-Paul 144
Tozzi, Romano 124
Tube 169
Tucker, Richard N. 402
Turell, Saul J. 440
Tyler, Parker 50, 170, 296, 313, 338, 387

Vance, James S. 102, 103
Vas, Robert 297
Vvoire (d'), Jean 468

Weinberg, Herman G. 403
Werb, 441
West, Anthony 171
Wharton, Flavia 172
Whitebait, William 51
Wissink, Charles Van 314
Wolf, Barbara 420

Yamada, Koji 284, 285
Yamamoto, Kikuo 339
Yodogawa, Choji 223
Young, Vernon 63, 64, 145, 388, 389

Zambrano, Ana Laura 421
Zendel, Jose 469
Zunser, Jesse 30, 390

Film Title Index

Akahige *see* Red Beard
Akira Kurosawa: Film Director 470
L'Ange ivre *see* Drunken Angel
Asu O Tsukuru Hitobito *see* Those Who Make Tomorrow

The Bad Sleep Well 160, 175-177, 179, 190, 192, 194, 197, 205, 211, 212, 264, 279, 331, 349, 431, 508, 512
Barbe rouge *see* Red Beard
Barberousse *see* Red Beard
Les bas-fonds *see* The Lower Depths
The Bodyguard *see* Yojimbo

The Castle of the Spider's Web *see* The Throne of Blood
Ceux qui bâtissent l'avenir *see* Those Who Make Tomorrow
Ceux qui font l'avenir *see* Those Who Make Tomorrow
Le chateau de l'araignée *see* The Throne of Blood
Le chien enragé *see* Stray Dog
Chronique d'un être vivant *see* Record of a Living Being
Cobweb Castle *see* The Throne of Blood

Dersu Uzala 414, 419, 425, 430, 439, 441-444, 446-448, 454
Director Kurosawa 502
Dodeskaden 318, 324, 330, 331, 335, 341-344, 346, 374, 376, 379, 404, 407, 408, 416, 417, 423, 432, 435, 438, 440, 508, 509
Dodesukaden *see* Dodeskaden
Donzoko *see* The Lower Depths
Doomed *see* Ikiru
Drunken Angel 56, 98, 104, 108, 117, 124, 331, 351, 375, 508, 509, 512
A Drunken Angel *see* Drunken Angel
Le duel silencieux *see* The Quiet Duel

Entre le ciel et l'enfre *see* High and Low

La forteresse cachée *see* The Hidden Fortress
La garde du corps *see* Yojimbo

Hakuchi *see* The Idiot
Heaven and Hell *see* High and Low
The Hidden Fortress 96, 101, 113, 114, 131, 137, 140, 141, 145, 154, 161, 228, 233, 250, 279, 310, 331, 349, 389, 504-506, 508, 509, 513
High and Low 178, 183, 189, 191, 196, 200, 206, 209, 213, 216, 218, 221, 228, 233, 236, 245, 251, 259, 264, 273, 279, 297, 502, 508, 514
Les hommes qui marchèrent sur la queue du tigre *see* The Men Who Tread on the Tiger's Tail

I Live in Fear *see* Record of a Living Being
Ichiban Utsukushiku *see* The Most Beautiful
The Idiot 188, 198, 204, 222, 228, 233, 234, 243, 284, 331, 348, 392, 393, 400, 401, 415, 417, 508, 509, 515
L'Idiot *see* The Idiot
Ikimono no Kiroku *see* Record of a Living Being
Ikiru 52, 75, 80, 83, 84, 99, 105, 106, 111, 112, 115, 118, 121, 122, 129, 139, 145, 166, 228, 233, 240, 279, 300, 331, 348, 417, 431, 437, 438, 505, 506, 508, 509

Je ne regrette pas ma jeunesse *see* No Regrets for Our Youth
Je ne regrette rien de ma jeunesse *see* No Regrets For Our Youth
Judo Saga — I *see* Sanshiro Sugata
Judo Saga — II *see* Sanshiro Sugata — Part Two

Kakushi Toride no San-Akunin *see* The Hidden Fortress
Kumonosu-Djo *see* The Throne of Blood
Kumonosu-jo *see* The Throne of Blood

La légende de judo — I see Sanshiro Sugata
La légende de judo — II see Sanshiro Sugata — Part Two
Living see Ikiru
The Lower Depths 102, 103, 149, 155, 158, 161, 164, 171, 172, 182, 213, 214, 279, 376, 379, 435, 452, 506, 508, 509, 512

Macbeth see The Throne of Blood
The Magnificent Seven see Seven Samurai
The Men Who Tread on the Tiger's Tail 85, 107, 109, 115, 116, 123, 171, 508, 509, 512
Un merveilleux dimanche see One Wonderful Sunday
The Most Beautiful 502, 508, 509
Most Beautifully see The Most Beautiful

Nora Inu see Stray Dog
No Regrets for My Youth see No Regrets for Our Youth
No Regrets for Our Youth 331, 340, 502, 508
Notes d'un être vivant see Record of a Living Being

One Wonderful Sunday 231, 331, 351, 438, 502, 508

Le paradis et l'enfer see High and Low
Le plus beau see The Most Beautiful
Le plus doux see The Most Beautiful

The Quiet Duel 331, 350, 431, 508, 512

The Ransom see High and Low
Rashomon 27, 28, 30-41, 45-55, 58, 61, 62, 64, 66, 70, 76, 86, 87, 97, 115, 139, 170, 171, 199, 228, 229, 233, 250a, 252a, 264, 265, 272, 289, 296, 305, 309, 312, 313, 338, 358-364, 366-371, 373, 378, 380, 381, 383, 387, 388, 390, 397, 406, 413, 433, 440, 445, 449, 458, 462, 464, 469, 494, 502-506, 508, 509
Record of a Living Being 173, 286, 288, 291, 424, 431, 512
Red Beard 249, 257, 262, 263, 267, 269, 270, 274, 277, 298, 301-303, 306, 308, 331, 352, 506, 508, 509, 512
The Rose in the Mud see The Bad Sleep Well

Les salauds dorment en paix see The Bad Sleep Well
Les salauds se portent bien see The Bad Sleep Well
Sanjuro 134, 169, 181, 185, 186, 193, 195, 207, 213, 252, 279, 345, 391, 436, 453, 458, 503, 508, 512
Sanshiro Sugata 56, 202, 252, 264, 277; 331, 340, 490, 496, 502, 503, 506, 508, 509, 512

Sanshiro Sugata — Part Two
Scandal 508, 512
Scandale see Scandal
Les sept samourais see Seven Samurai
Seven Samurai 56, 58, 60, 66-74, 76, 77, 79, 82, 85, 97, 121, 127, 134a, 140, 145, 152, 239, 250a, 322, 328, 372, 420, 424, 436, 458, 461, 468, 493, 502, 505-507, 508, 511, 512
Shichinin no Samurai see Seven Samurai
Shizukanaru Ketto see The Quiet Duel
Shubun see Scandal
A Silent Duel see The Quiet Duel
Si les oiseaux savaient see Record of a Living Being
Stray Dog 49, 216, 219, 225-227, 230, 232, 238, 253, 259, 273, 314, 331, 350, 502, 508, 512
Subarashiki Nichiyobi see One Wonderful Sunday
Sugata Sanshiro see Sanshiro Sugata
Sur la queue du tigre see The Men Who Tread on the Tiger's Tail

Tengoku to Jigoku see High and Low
They Who Step on the Tiger's Tail see The Men Who Tread on the Tiger's Tail
Three Bad Men in a Hidden Fortress see The Hidden Fortress
Those Who Make Tomorrow 502, 508
The Throne of Blood 86, 90, 91, 93, 94, 125-128, 129, 130, 132, 135, 138, 140, 153, 171, 187, 213, 228, 233, 235, 260, 261, 279, 295, 307, 310, 315, 316, 353, 394, 395, 399, 409, 421, 424, 455, 458, 502, 506-508, 512
To Live see Ikiru
Tora no O o Fumu Otokotachi see The Men Who Tread on the Tiger's Tail
Trois salauds dans une forteresse cachée see The Hidden Fortress
Le trône sanglant see The Throne of Blood
Tsubaki Sanjuro see Sanjuro

Vivre see Ikiru
Vivre dans la peur see Record of a Living Being
Vivre enfin un seul jour see Ikiru

Waga Seishun ni Kuinashi see No Regrets for Our Youth
Walkers on the Tiger's Tail see The Men Who Tread on the Tiger's Tail
Warui Yatsu Hodo Yoku Nemuru see The Bad Sleep Well
What the Birds Knew see Record of a Living Being
Wonderful Sunday see One Wonderful Sunday
The Worse You are the Better You Sleep see The Bad Sleep Well

Yoidore Tenshi *see* Drunken Angel
Yojimbo 133, 134, 144, 146, 148, 150, 151, 156, 157, 159, 162, 163, 165, 203, 213, 266, 275, 279, 310, 319, 372, 391, 411, 424, 426, 431, 436, 458, 495, 504, 508, 509, 512